To Teeruck

Many thanks for your support with Leadership S.O. It is greatly appreciated.

Many thanks

Best

Paul

Leadership 5.0

The Future of Leadership

Paul Corke

First published in Great Britain in 2022
by Amazon Publishing

© Copyright Paul Corke 2022

The moral right of Paul Corke to be identified as the author of this work has been asserted in accordance with the Copyright, Designs and Patents Acts 1988.

All rights reserved. No part of this publication may be reproduced, stored in a retrieval system, or transmitted, in any form or by any means without the prior written permission of the publisher, nor be otherwise circulated in any form of binding or cover than that in which it is published and without similar condition being imposed on the subsequent purchaser.

The Quadrant Model of Leadership on page 30 (c) Paul Corke 2022

ISBN 9798351237213

Reviewed and edited by Olivia Eisinger & Cover Design by Lee Deakin.

About the Author

Paul Corke is an author, keynote speaker, and thought leader, considered to be a leading expert on mindset, innovation, and leadership. He is currently recognised as No 1 Health and Wellness Thought Leader & Influencer with @Thinkers360.

He has previously spent 25 years in the corporate world with award-winning results, specialising in organisational effectiveness, employee engagement, talent management and leadership development with experience in UK, Ireland, Europe, US, and the Middle East.

More recently he was the Managing Director of Leadership Innovators an innovative leadership development consultancy with a niche specialism in leadership model design, thought leadership, leadership development strategy, leadership assessment, coaching and solutions.

Paul is the author of 'Reframe Your Mindset: Redefine Your Success', has a podcast series to support the book and has created 'The Mindset Journal', all based on what he calls 'The Mindset Equation for Success.' Paul also uses his research into mindset and positive psychology along with the thinking from his books, to provide thought leadership and solutions to help organisations build their leadership capability.

Paul has successfully built leadership development strategies and provided solutions in the Financial Services, Retail, Automobile, Charity, Mass Media, Healthcare and Information Technology industries, as well as in Education, Humanitarian and Local Government.

His mission is to develop leaders the world now wants to see, whilst also making a difference through B1G1, working towards the UN Global Strategic Development Goals to help those in need across the world.

Currently recognised as…

- *No 1 Health & Wellness Thought Leader and Influencer 2021 & 2022 with Thinkers360*
- *Top 50 HR Thinkers for 2021 with Thinkers360*
- *Passion Vista Men Leaders to Look Up to in 2021*
- *Brainz Global 500 Leaders 2021 for Entrepreneurship, Achieving Results and Helping Others*
- *B1G1 World's Most Inspiring Businesses for Paul Corke International*

Publications

- *Reframe Your Mindset: Redefine Your Success*
- *The Master: In Search of Meaning & Purpose*
- *The Master: Developing Psychological Intelligence*
- *The New Positive Thinking: Develop Your Mindset to Shape Your Future*
- *Co-Author of the #1 Amazon Best Seller - Resilient Voices*
- *Leadership 5.0: The Future of Leadership*

Contents

Testimonials 6

Introduction 9

Prologue 13

1 The Present 26

2 Time Travel to the Past 40

3 Megatrends of the Future 63

4 Redefining Leadership 83

5 A Leader's Mindset 101

6 The Mindset of an Organisation 124

7 Culture 138

8 The Future of Leadership 152

9 Leadership Development 176

10 Beyond Leadership 197

References and Further Reading 208

Endorsement for Leadership 5.0: The Future of Leadership

"A must-read for all leaders aspiring to take their leadership to the next dimension: future-prepared, resilient and built for growth."

- Terence Mauri, Founder Hack Future Lab and Visiting Professor, IE Business School

"In a world where there are some many unique and serious challenges, we need a new type of leader. Paul's latest book, Leadership 5.0, provides the blueprint for this. Leadership 5.0 is a fantastic, but crucially, a very important book which every leader should read."

- Neil Francis, Author of Changing Course

"The world desperately needs better leaders. And this book shows you how to be one of them."

- Steve Pipe – Author of Our time to RISE

"I write this testimonial for Paul's latest book on the day following Boris Johnson's resignation as Leader of the Conservative Party and Prime Minster. It therefore perhaps an excellent time to reflect on leadership and what is we expect from our leaders. Paul book is both an excellent summary of academic theories on leadership as well as an historical exploration of the prevailing leadership styles over the last 2000 years. I particularly like how he cross referenced leadership to the animal kingdom. As you would expect Paul is not only thoughtful and inspiring, but he is also very much future focused, identifying the leadership styles that will be required for the challenges ahead. He describes at some length values based, human centred and purposeful leadership. He also explores the mindsets that will be required to develop the next generation of these leaders. And of course, as always he makes reference to sport. I can commend this book to you without reservation."

- Michael Moran, CEO of 10Eighty

"Leadership 5.0 is an important book at the right moment. Never before have we needed leaders with a new level of thinking and understanding in the post-pandemic world. It is a time for the spirit of creativity and innovation in leadership to show itself. Paul Corke has produced an imaginative and timely text in tune with the times."

- Trevor Merriden, Thought Leader and MD at Merriborn Media

"As the world changes around us, the nature of leadership and what it means to be a leader is also evolving. Corke's book fills a nice gap in the research about why change is happening and what the new mindset for leaders needs to be. It is written in an accessible style, blending stories, examples from a range of sources and drawing on leading thinking and research, and contains a range of practical questions for leaders and organisations to answer. If you want to lead effectively in the new world of work, read this first – it'll tell you what is different, why it is different and help you to reflect on whether you want to and know how to be that difference."

- Gary Cookson, Author of HR for Hybrid Working and Director at EPIC

"Yet once again another an amazing work from Paul Corke, Leadership 5.0. I would say I truly enjoyed reading this as Paul did showcase how leadership has evolved & how leadership needs to be changed to the future. From leaders' control to leaders role to elevate leaders, such a powerful thought process has gone into the book.

Furthermore, Paul has perfectly articulated the present challenges (Climate crisis, Scarcity of resources etc) the world is facing & connected to the elements of leadership. With the global pandemic we all went through to virtual working, Paul has done amazing work around human centered leadership to overcome challenges in virtual & hybrid working environment.

Further he does elaborate on different mindsets which is an eye opener. One of my favorite parts of this book is how Paul has reflected on the lesson from Animals, It is a very thought provoking approach. This book is highly recommended to all level of employee in an organization as it covers a holistic approach to leadership."

- Azeem Saheer, Human Capital Specialist- Facilitator at Luminary Learning Solution & EQ Leadership Coach, Emotional Culture Catalyst, Speaker & Podcaster

Introduction

The End of the World as We Know it

Why we need to take our burning platform seriously...

> *"What the caterpillar calls the end of the world, the master calls butterfly."*
> *– Richard Bach, American writer*

Right now, our burning platform as a human race is...

The survival of the human race.

When we think of the Bible and the end of the world, there is the vision of the Four Riders of the Apocalypse. The fact is those four riders are rapidly approaching humankind in the form of destructive megatrends that will shape the future of our world. We will need to evolve and adapt at a greater pace than ever before, because exponential change is happening even faster than we anticipated.

Who are those Four Riders of the Apocalypse?

I dare to rename them from Conquest, War, Famine and Plague to...Climate Change, Pandemic, Scarcity of Resources and War/Terrorism.

If we do not take them seriously, these megatrends will spell doom for all of us and they will wreak havoc across the Earth if unchecked. We have a responsibility to tackle these riders head on, to ensure not only human survival but also that we protect all living things on this planet at the same time.

"Doom mongering!" I can hear you say... a little perhaps, but let's take the facts into consideration.

- The Earth is heating up - according to NOAA's 2020 Annual Climate Report, the combined land and ocean temperature has increased at an average rate of 0.13 degrees Fahrenheit (0.08 degrees Celsius) per decade since 1880; however, the average rate of increase since 1981 (0.18°C / 0.32°F) has been more than twice that rate.

- The Food and Agriculture Organisation of the United Nations is predicting that by 2025, 1.8 billion people will be living in countries or regions with absolute water scarcity.

- The BP Statistical Review of World Energy in June 2021, measured total global oil at 188.8 million tonnes, from proved oil resources at the end of 2010. This is only enough to oil for the next 46.2 years, should global production remain at the current rate.

- A similar picture to oil exists for natural gas, with enough gas in proven reserves at the end of 2010 to meet 58.6 years of global production.

- With the need to feed 7 billion people, scientists from the Global Phosphorus Research Initiative predict we could run out of phosphorus in 50 to 100 years, unless new reserves of the element are found.

- Inequality has reached unprecedented levels, with more than 70% of the global population living in countries where the wealth gap is growing, according to a new UN report.

- In fact, sea levels have risen faster over the last hundred years than any time in the last 3,000 years. This acceleration is expected to continue. A further 15-25cm of sea level rise is expected by 2050, with little sensitivity to greenhouse gas emissions between now and then.

- COVID-19 is broadly viewed as being a "once in a lifetime" or "once in a century" pandemic. CGD modelling work based on historical data shows that this is not necessarily the case.

- As I write this, Russian troops, tanks and military army are being deployed into and devasting Ukraine, destabilising peace with the West – worrying times that this new Cold War could lead to the next World War.

- And terrorism continues wave after wave, after Sept 11th, 2001, with the destruction of the Twin Towers. Terrorism has not gone away as we all know, and it will continue to plague the Earth with the worries of bio-terrorism amongst new and deadlier ways to inflict pain across the globe.

All a bit negative to start a book when I could start with the technological advances, new innovative thinking, humankind's creativity, and curiosity that are also shaping the future, but a reality check is always a good place to start.

I'm an optimist! I believe we have the internal resources and know how to adapt and survive. I believe if we work together instead of apart, we can meet these new challenges head on, but they will take the tenacity, human spirit and most importantly, the collaboration across cultures and international boundaries to ensure we survive.

Never before have we needed leaders to be the leaders the world now wants to see. In the future, we will need a new level of thinking and understanding about leadership in a world of constant change and where human becomes wired as society becomes fully interconnected. Where technology and AI will completely disrupt our way of life, to then become a natural part of the way we live.

Soon generations will not know any different.

And also, a future where we will become more aware of our past, a past that defies current timelines to point to a more sophisticated understanding of who we are.

Apocalypse perhaps not, reawakening perhaps so… the stage is set.

"The future depends upon what we do in the present." –
Mahatma Gandhi, author and civil rights leader who preached non-violence

Prologue

What we know...

A high-level view of how leadership has developed...

> "People buy into the leader before they buy into the vision." - John Maxwell, American writer and speaker

I have always been interested in both the past and the future but mindful to live my life in the present. It is difficult not to want to explore the past to identify our origins, or in this case, how leadership has developed in the past to shape the here and now. To understand how we have been conditioned by what has come before. But I also have a massive interest in the future and how technological marvels will come to bear as well as being interested in how we will cope due to climate change, the recent pandemic and possibility of further destructive forces that could impact the Earth.

This book is a journey into leadership and into how organisations will need to adapt in the future. I explore the past, present, and future, so we understand what has come before and how it will impact us now, but also to explore the forces at play that make life in the future more unpredictable than it has been in the past.

We will explore the different ages of humankind to see what we have learnt when it comes to leadership, and if we have truly learned what it takes to be a great leader. More so, how leadership is changing and how collaboration will be key to our success in the future.

From my own experience of the corporate world and business, I will share experiences and observations along with the insights from great leaders who I have been fortunate to stand on the shoulders of and learn from, to be able to shape my leadership. And like many, I have personally led well in some situations and organisations and not so well in others, but I have learnt from it and will share some of those insights as we explore a new paradigm of leadership.

What can we learn from the leadership of other species on the Earth in how they lead, collaborate, and build teams, which at times are far more effective than human teams?

When we think of leaders or leadership do, we think of world leaders, past leaders, political leaders, war time leaders, ancient leaders, organisational leaders, leaders from the world of sport or the many more examples that can be as simple as experiences through work, friends, and family.

Leaders have that innate ability to be able to lead as a visionary but also the charisma that means people will follow them. We can describe leadership in lots of different ways, and I intend to explore the different levels of leadership and how we are still continually looking to move away from command-and-control style leadership in organisations. I aim to provide different ways of thinking about leadership whilst also providing a view of leadership in the future.

But let's start with some leadership context...

When I was working in the corporate world, I worked for a brilliant CEO whose definition of leadership was...

> *'Leadership is about making a choice to stand for something, it is a deliberate decision, and it is a visible demonstration.'*

This is a great starting point for defining leadership, a leader's motivation, and the importance of being a visible leader, especially in a changing world where most people are now led remotely due to the recent pandemic outbreak. This has brought new challenges for leaders which we will discuss.

As the world is changing, leaders face a multitude of new challenges and megatrends so there is more to leadership than making a choice, but it is obviously a great starting point. Especially if you do stand up for something you believe in. Manville & Ober (2003) describe how our managerial and governance systems are now outdated, coming from the Industrial Era and how we are now in the Knowledge Era with exponential technological change and growing uncertainty in the workplace, with new expectations of leaders. From a hierarchical perspective, there has always been command-and-control leadership where the boss, manager or leader holds the power and exerts that power to lead.

The Great Man Theory

In the 1840s, Thomas Carlyle proposed the Great Man Theory, the concept that leaders are born with inherent traits that will make them great leaders. He stated, "The history of the world is but the biography of great men." And according to Carlyle, it was those men who were gifted with the right traits and characteristics from birth. With no scientific proof, the theory advocated that leadership could not be learned because it was a built-in trait. Over the generations, this has sparked the conversation about our leaders; are they born or are they made? The theory was heavily criticised over the years as being a male-centric approach which neglects situational factors that impact leadership.

Sociologist Herbert Spencer's view suggests leaders are a product of societal influences, in his 1873 book, *'The Study of Sociology'*. "You must admit that the genesis of a great man depends on the long series of complex influences which has produced the race in which he appears, and the social state into which that race has slowly grown… Before he can remake his society, his society must make him."

But back in the 1800s, leadership was in general seen as being something you were born to do or being in a position of power, instead of being possible to develop, and the working structure of industrial society reinforced the theory at the time.

Coercive Leadership

Drucker (1998) says that the basic assumptions made about management are out of date and those assumptions have outlived their time. If we go back to the Industrial Age, leadership was defined by the power in the relationship i.e., the boss or manager had dictatorial power over the worker. This level of conditioning meant that defiant leadership was embedded within early organisations so you as the boss could stand for something, but the means or methods of leadership would be less engaging for the worker. Because quite simply, they were being told what to do. And although we have seen a move away from coercive leadership styles in Western culture, there are still many countries who have a more coercive style of leadership in the workplace. In a recent study by Hays Group covering 95,000 leaders in over 2,200 organisations across the world, 62% of leaders in India were found to be using the 'coercive' style of leadership, impacting culture and innovation.

Transactional Leadership

If we look back 20 years ago in the US and UK for example, leadership was more transactional, where the power relationship shifted to agreed beneficial transactions between the worker and leadership, to achieve desired task outcomes together. Max Weber, a 20th-century German sociologist, completed extensive research into leadership styles and was first to describe transactional leadership as "the exercise of control on the basis of knowledge."

Transactional leadership theory is based on the idea that managers give employees something they want, in exchange for getting something in return. For example, employees are given benefits and incentives and in return they are expected to achieve challenging sales targets. The transactional leadership style was widely used after World War II and has continued into modern office times, but as Hernez-Broome & Hughes (2012) stress, 'The exchange-model nature of transactional leadership tends to produce predictable and somewhat short-lived outcomes.'

Transactional leadership is all about give and take but lacks any inspiration or real motivation to do more or be more. This plays out in workplace situations where an individual just wants a job but not so much a career. When more of us worked in factories, this worked really well, but in the more modern and complex settings of today, the relationship over time with little inspiration, will be short-lived.

Leadership Styles

Peltier (2010, p312-313) describes three classical leadership styles from an experiment by Kurt Lewin, as Autocratic, Democratic and Laissez-Faire Leadership styles, of which Kotter (1999) says, 'Style is not the key leadership issue. Substance is.' Leadership through the generations have been defined by the power in the relationship between the manager and worker. What we mean by leadership now in the Knowledge Era requires both style and substance, along with new ways of thinking.

What a Leader Should Be

Adair (2005) explains there are three Approaches to understanding leadership. The first is the 'Qualities Approach' which asks, 'What a Leader should be', creating desired qualities, so is in some respects, a Leadership Brand. The second way to understand leadership is the 'Situational Approach' which asks, 'What a leader has to do or know.' And the third and final way is the 'Group or Functional Analysis Approach' which focuses on the Leader's job to address three group needs – to achieve goals, the needs of the group and the needs of individuals. This can be an effective way in breaking down what a leader's role is within organisations with a focus on 'What' needs to be achieved and the 'How' behaviours of leaders.

One of the main messages from Adair's book, *'How to Grow Leaders: – the seven principles of effective leadership development'* is 'The basic principle in leadership development is that an organisation should never give a team leadership role or position to someone without training.' Adair feels every organisation must develop future leaders.

The Leadership Challenge

In *'The Leadership Challenge'* by Posner and Kouzes (1995), they believe that leadership is not a generic trait, and anyone can be a leader. They completed research with almost 1,400 leaders to identify five fundamental practices effective leaders follow: 1. Challenge the process 2. Inspire a shared vision 3. Enable others to act 4. Set an example and 5. Encourage the heart. They believe that everything taught in management circles is wrong and the first challenge a leader faces is getting rid of flawed notions about what a leader really is. Leaders who exert control or who exaggerate their position struggle to build trust and achieve their objectives. The key message is leadership is for the many, not the few.

Authentic Leadership

Bill George in 'Authentic Leadership' (2003) feels Enron and WorldCom did the world a favour by ensuring the focus on the problems of capitalism have now shown us that a new form of authentic leadership is required, built on integrity and ethics. George says true leadership can only begin when leaders look deep into themselves and see who they really are and if they really want to be leaders. Real leadership is honest, true, deep, insightful, purposeful, and motivated by high ideals. Leaders must be true to themselves. Authentic leaders have five traits: to know themselves, act with integrity, do what is right, avoid greed, think long term, and demand no more from others than they expect from themselves.

In essence, a leader has integrity and respect based on their values of doing what is right in the world. But whose predetermined version of what is right is correct?

We all see the world differently, which is why we sometimes have conflict between people. However, if we act with integrity and respect to all people with a level of authenticity, it is now an essential factor of what good looks like for leadership in the 21st century.

As we see with world leaders, governments, and politicians, the use of manipulation, lies, and trickery has become the new norm. The authenticity of being a complete scoundrel (without naming names), is not what the world needs, but instead, an authenticity which is a force for good rather than selfish desires and self-interest.

Emotional Intelligence

Goleman (2002) states that great leaders lead emotionally, and leaders should be inspiring. He defines six leadership styles, four are positive and create resonance and two are negative and are at high risk of dissonance.

- The positive styles are Visionary, Coaching, Affiliative and Democratic
- The negative are Pacesetting and Commanding.

Emotional control is an essential element in today's working environment and being able to motivate and inspire takes a level of emotional intelligence to connect with others. It has been proven leaders with a high IQ or subject matter experts tend not to lead as well as those with high EQ. A balance of both will always help with one's credibility as a leader.

Transformational Leadership

Leadership expert James MacGregor Burns introduced the concept of transformational leadership in his 1978 book, "Leadership." He defined it as a process where "leaders and their followers raise one another to higher levels of morality and motivation."

Transformational leadership, in comparison to Transactional Leadership as Bass (1985) explains, is about self-awareness, transcendence, and a level of charisma.

Transformational leadership is where a leader goes beyond their immediate self-interests to create a vision, provide inspiration, and take their followers with them in pursuit of that vision. People follow transactional leaders because they have to, but with transformational leadership they follow because they **want** to.

Learning Styles

Lyons (2012) says 'Different people like different learning styles' in Goldsmith, Lyons, & Freas, '*Coaching for Leadership: How the World's Greatest Coaches Help Leaders Learn.*' This means that the leader as a coach should learn theory, tools, and techniques to match them appropriate to their team member, the coachee. Lyons also suggests that leaders who inspire coachees to link their work to their personal development and to the vision of the company, will then have 'purposeful connectedness'. Lyons sums it up as a balance between the career and personal development of the individual, but also understanding the role they play in the company's mission for the greater good of society or the customer.

The Leadership Coaching Revolution

What is essential when it comes to coaching on leadership, is an understanding of the many leadership theories. Peltier (2010) says 'Effective coaches must be intimately familiar with the leadership literature, leadership theory and prominent models,' in his book *The Psychology of Executive Coaching: Theory and Application.*' But how many leaders turn up and manage based on the way they were managed or lead, without any study into leadership best practice and theory?

Leaders Create Leaders, Not Followers

The most profound statement on leadership is from Peters (2004): *'Leaders do not create followers; they create more leaders.'* This is where we should land if we talk about leadership now, that leaders should have the knowledge, skills, and capability to create leaders in their own right. Everyone is a leader, so creating leaders and not followers, is the current paradigm that I will look to promote in this book, but also go beyond, as we explore leadership in the future.

In general, the organisations and industries I have worked in have been inherently command-and-control centres, with others having pockets of it scattered across the business. When we understand the organisational context, we really get an insight into the organisational conditioning, so the longer you are in an organisation, the more likely you are to be institutionalised. The same is true with most leaders-in-waiting; if not provided with the right level of training, coaching and support, they will copy their manager when they become the new leader. This then is the lottery of leadership. If they are good then great, but if not, then dysfunctional leadership will seep through the organisation and over long periods of time can have devastating effects on the company.

Individuals will quickly start to see the mindset of the organisation through its leaders, even if it is not what the organisation intends. Direct experience day in, day out, speaks more volumes than words on a poster stating company values. If the leaders do not live and breathe these values, the impacts will speak for themselves and vice versa. So being able to coach leaders to develop a visionary, coaching and facilitative style of leadership is essential in developing the leaders of the future, whilst challenging beliefs and assumptions to drive behavioural change.

Outliers

There will always be outliers when it comes to leadership. When we talk about transformational leadership and coaching, some people do prefer to be told what to do and not think for themselves. This is why it takes a range of leadership styles to be able to manage a group of people, and self-awareness as a leader to be able to connect and apply those techniques or styles.

Have you have seen *Lessons on Leadership* from a Dancing Guy (if you have not seen it, then search YouTube)? At a festival one lone nut gets up to start crazy dancing and most people look at him like he is an idiot, but then he gets his first follower. This is a pivotal moment because everything then changes. Then another joins, and another, until eventually you are the odd one out if you are not dancing with the group. The lesson? Well, if no-one had got up to dance then he would have looked like that lone nut on the hill, the nerd without a cause and no lesson in leadership gained.

But in fact, he was able to create a movement and it was actually the first follower that changed everything that gave his cause momentum to make the movement happen. Accidental leadership - in this situation the first follower should be credited for creating the movement. Watch it and consider how it challenges the leadership norm but also brilliantly challenges the importance of followership.

There is also the debate of who makes a good leader and if it is nature or nurture but what we now understand is that leaders can be made, and leadership can be learnt. However, there is no recipe or place you will find leaders. Some of the best leaders have been those who have created a movement such as Gandhi or Nelson Mandela; they are not always stereotypical leaders in their style and essence but have achieved amazing feats through their persistence and beliefs.

> *"Leaders are found in the strangest places. Often the best candidates turn out to be people from outside the mainstream - - the misfits, the critics, sometimes even the naysayers -- who at first glance one would never expect would have leadership potential. So be prepared to look for new leaders in unexpected places and to give them the opportunity they need." - Dov Frohman, Israeli author*

And as we know, the world is changing at such a rapid pace, replacing mechanical jobs or the jobs of those who do not want to think for themselves, that we will have little time. Will there be a need for leadership in the future? And, then there are the outliers that happen to us, none more so than what started a couple of years ago, when the whole world changed with the onset of COVID 19 and the onset of working from home during lockdown and new ways of working were thrust upon most of us.

This in itself requires new leadership, to be able to manage remotely and face to face at the same time. Yes, some were ahead of the curve, but many were not, so exponential change, which was already happening, doubled in pace. And with megatrends and the Four Riders of the Apocalypse, we have never needed more to develop the leaders the world now wants to see. So where are we now?

1
The Present

Where are we right now?

Has leadership kept up with the rate of change?

> "As we look to the next century, leaders will be those who empower others."
> - Bill Gates, American business magnate

In 1847, Dr. Ignaz Semmelweis's discovered his friend Jakob Kolletschka caught a nasty disease known as puerperal fever. Semmelweis also made the correlation that 13% of new mothers died of the fever in the local training hospital in Vienna but the nearby local hospital only lost 2%. Semmelweis observed that the difference was the students where not washing their hands when entering and exiting the theatre room. He asked the students to wash their hands in a chlorine solution and the mortality rate dropped to 2%.

Sadly, the medical establishment rejected his ideas but eventually Joseph Lister learning of Semmelweis' work began to use carbolic acid as a disinfectant and achieved the same the results. He credited Semmelweis for the discovery, but sadly it was too late for Semmelweis; he had passed away after being discredited in a mental institution.

Semmelweis also gave his name to the 'Semmelweis Effect', a metaphor where new research or evidence is rejected because it contradicts established norms and beliefs and current ways of thinking.

As human beings, we tend to become conditioned by past thinking and also inherently conform to what is seen as the norm. At times this makes new discoveries which challenge existing paradigms difficult to become accepted across society.

Slightly different to actually basing new ways of thinking on research and evidence, are predictions for the future. If we won't believe new ideas based on empirical evidence, then why would we listen to suggestions about the future? But if I were to ask you what are your predictions for the future, how accurate do you think you would be? Would you be able to predict the megatrends, their impacts and when they will happen?

We can all predict the predictable, but who actually predicted the recent global pandemic we have all faced that literally changed the face of the Earth overnight? What we have recently experienced has sped up the future in the ways that we work, where we work from, access to jobs and talent, and the way we think about life. It's challenged our principles and made us appreciate what we had, made some more fearful, and as a whole, has been a complete paradigm change in how we think about the world.

In his Ted Talk in 2015, Bill Gates said the world needs to prepare for a pandemic the way it prepares for war, and that we were not ready for the next pandemic outbreak. The billionaire has been warning of a pandemic for years, as have disease and flu experts. In a recent interview, he said the next big disasters facing humanity are climate change and bio-terrorism. And with the chances of the existing Coronavirus mutating along with further pandemics, the reality is that our world will never be the same. And, of course, with each disaster of epic proportions, the poverty gap is widening across the globe.

The Evolution of Leadership

When we think about all the change in the world we have experienced in the last 20 years and the advances in the fields of technology, AI, and automation, we are on the cusp of living in a new era - The 'Human Age'- along with meeting the demands of future generations' expectations in the workplace which are changing with each generation. And when we think of all the change that has happened and is happening around us, has leadership evolved at the same pace? What is leadership now? Has it kept up with the advances in the world, with the pandemic and developed across global organisations? Are the same leadership qualities required as before?

Eddie Obeng in his TED Talk, describes the 'World after Midnight'; at some point around 15-20 years ago there was a reset point (Midnight), where the rate of human learning no longer kept up with technological change. Has leadership evolved in the last 20 years? Or has it suffered from the Semmelweis Effect?

Recently I read an article on Leadership in the Future, where the writer was challenged on where they currently see leadership. The challenger's point was "I'm not sure what industries you have been working in, but I'm still seeing hierarchical, political, command-and-control leadership across the organisations I partner with."

The spectrum of leadership exists, and we can place organisations across the spectrum as to where their leadership is right now. But then within any business, there will be pockets of leaders who inspire, empower, and motivate, while others use coercive command and control. In a recent Gallup study, it is claimed that 50% of employees are not engaged and 25% are disengaged, so this in itself provides possible evidence that Leadership is not keeping up with new generational demands of our current workforce.

Although I appreciate there are many factors that can lead to employee dissatisfaction, what we do know is that most people will become disengaged and leave their job due to their manager. I'm pretty sure that if you have an employee survey, each year there will be leadership actions and development that comes from the survey. And that is if your workforce feel they can freely speak their mind. Another leadership conundrum...

In any medium to large organisation there will be an inertia and level of organisational conditioning which means there will be certain expectations of how to lead in the organisation. These expectations at times become deeply embedded in the leader's subconscious, so much so that no-one has actually made the rules but believe there to be rules they need to follow. No one challenges those invisible rules, and everyone continues to conform. Action, or lack of action, is then in direct proportion to conditioning. The senior leadership team will model either exemplary or dysfunctional behaviours which then shape the company culture; the by product is the need to lead and manage in the same way to conform to acceptable standards. We are creatures of habit and comfort, so rather than choosing to swim upstream, most will conform and not challenge dysfunctional behaviours or a dysfunctional culture.

Leaders can at times treat their people like children instead of like adults, and although they know they should not do this, if the rules of work state something different they can execute this against what would be their own personal beliefs. Power and conformity overcome common sense. Organisational conditioning takes a hold when leaders are not willing to challenge the norm. At a higher level in some board rooms the Execs play out a power struggle and some may display more dysfunctional behaviour than the people they have working for them. Sometimes the badge of hierarchy dictates when it should listen.

To also understand leadership, you have to tap into the mindset of the working population first and identify what it is your people really want from you as a leader, and how has this changed since lockdown and pandemic.

"Over half of the employees want to leave [their jobs], and there's really two reasons that came out of the survey," Catalyst President and CEO Lorraine Hariton tells CNBC's Julia Boorstin.

"One is if they felt that their employers did not understand them, that they weren't providing empathy. This is especially true for working parents, male or female. They didn't feel good about the experience, and they're looking to leave. The second thing is that people are really leaning into flexibility, whether that's flexibility by location, by when they work, or how they work. They want to leave if the employer is not providing that."

So right now, most workers want flexibility in how they work in the way that remote working during the pandemic provided and proved that it could work. Many workers are giving up their high-rate mortgages and rent to move out of the cities into the countryside, because they can now work from anywhere. In fact, smart working is now the new expectation of a lot of workers, who now understand they can work from anywhere in the world.

When organisations think about designing the future work experience, those organisations that provide flexibility through remote, hybrid and smart working options and who experiment to get this right will be ahead of the curve. Businesses who get this right will likely attract and retain the best talent, and that talent pool will be much wider than was previously available.

Employees want:

1. flexibility in where they work
2. autonomy & empowerment
3. variety
4. balance
5. to be decision-makers and shapers
6. to be treated like professionals
7. to be leaders

We are also led to understand that wants and needs are different based on generational differences. Baby Boomers (born 1946–1964) want phased retirement, part-time work and health benefits, Generation X (born 1965–1980) want independence and flexibility, Millennials (born 1981–1995) want job stability and career development, Generation Z (born 1996–2010) want financial support and mental health support. Post pandemic Millennials and Gen X are more interested in a hybrid home-office work environment post-pandemic, to balance family obligations, while Boomers and Gen Z want to spend more time in the office to benefit from in-person connections and collaboration. What we do understand is that it takes a leadership style that is contextual to be able to deal with diversity and needs of different generations and people.

In a massive study by the Hay Group, researchers analysed data from over 5 million employees across the world to make comparisons across different generations. What they found was that generational differences are more likely to reflect the stage of development of employees, as opposed to their generation.

Rather than focusing on developing "generation specific" skills, and defining people's needs at work by gender, age, or cultural background, today's leaders should "be able to flex and adapt leadership styles to the needs of each individual."

Ikigai

What most employees really want is to find some kind of meaning and purpose for what they do. In *'Ikigai: The Japanese Secret to a Long and Happy Life'* by Hector Garcia, he reveals it is important to do what you love and what you are good at matched to what the world needs, and what you can get paid for.

The book was reviewed by the Guardian as *"The Japanese art of Ikigai ... Its basic message is about "authentic living". Practitioners must fill in overlapping circles that cover motivation, fulfilment, what they earn and what improves their life. The answer at the centre will be the key to a happy and long life".*

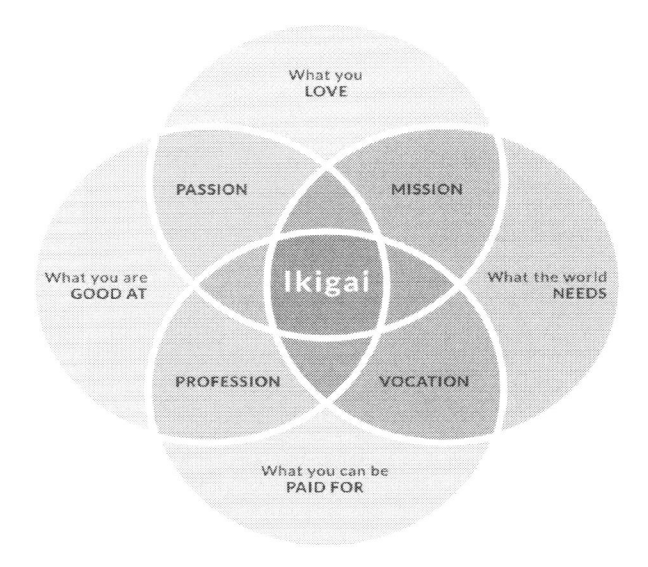

Image from: https://www.forbes.com/sites/chrismyers/2018/02/23/how-to-find-your-ikigai-and-transform-your-outlook-on-life-and-business/?sh=49164dbd2ed4

People have now realised since the pandemic the importance of balance, flexibility and what is important in life. Hence why we have seen the great resignation across the globe as people look for new ways of working to suit their lifestyle, instead of the other way round. The power is now firmly back with the employee with talent available remotely across the world.

So, has leadership kept up with the pace of change in the world?

The Spectrum of Leadership

If you were to rate yourself on the spectrum of leadership below, where would it be? And why?

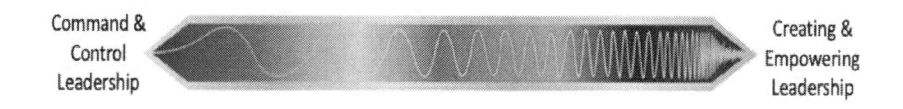

Command & Control Leadership ⟷ Creating & Empowering Leadership

If you were to rate your organisation on the spectrum of leadership, where would the organisation be? And why?

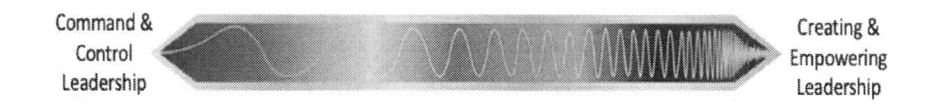

Command & Control Leadership ⟷ Creating & Empowering Leadership

Leadership 1.0. **Leaders are in control and dictate** (Hierarchical Command-and-Control Leadership).

Leadership 2.0. **Leaders transact with their people** (Transactional Leadership – I give you something i.e. an incentive, and you give me something in return).

Leadership 3.0. **Leaders inspire and create followers** (Transformational Leadership – people follow you because they are inspired and want to follow you).

Leadership 4.0. **Leaders create leaders** (Creational Leadership – Leaders give their people the confidence and autonomy to be the leader they are).

Leadership 5.0. **Leaders elevate leaders** (Autonomous Leadership – Leaders elevate and connect leaders who are purposeful, contextual, human-centred neuroleaders to create agile and powerful hive-style leadership and make a difference in the world).

For the day and age that we live in, we might surmise we are playing at the Transformational, Creational and Autonomous leadership levels, where employees are empowered and treated like leaders in their own right. If that is the case, then your organisation is possibly keeping up with the rate of change in the world and will be ready to meet the expectations of the generations to come. As generations in the future will be doing more sophisticated work as AI and automation takes over the manual processes, their expectation set point will be to be treated as a leader and given freedom to express themselves.

Work in the future is more likely to be episodic so one may move from one organisation to the next more frequently but one's expectation will be to be treated as a leader not as an employee. Josh Bersin from Deloitte talked recently about how the employee and organisation relationship will completely change due to expectations of the generations to come, with impacts such as the recent pandemic completely changing the landscape. And HR faces an inflection point around becoming career and people-focused as opposed to performance and company-focused. But then I don't want to move too far into the future because this chapter is about leadership now and understanding if it has evolved to keep up with the rate of change in the present.

What keeps leaders up at night?

Lack of talent, the challenge of remote working, the digital tech space, lack of critical skills, employees' lack of digital experience, automation at work and an aging workforce, according to Mercer's Global Talent Trends. So we have to accept that leadership is far more complex than 20 years ago, especially when leadership was most of the time face to face line management. Whereas in this day and age, you are a leader as an individual contributor. When responsible for people as a line manager, the expectation is now remote leadership across the globe along with agile working practices.

According to Mercer's Trends, 96% of executives are planning structural changes and unique human skills are most in demand i.e. innovation, digital competence, global mindset, data analysis, complex problem-solving, change and inclusive leadership. We also now see a greater talent vacuum, where desirable skills in specific niche areas are not readily available and therefore organisations are embracing exponential learning to upskill, upgrade and provide development experiences to their employees.

Those organisations that have now moved to hybrid or remote working as their new normal, will be able to tap into a more diverse and wider talent pool than before across the world as required.

The requirements and expectations of a leader have definitely changed. The landscape has changed as we face the burning platform that the pandemic has created but the question has to be, do leaders in your organisation understand what 'good' looks like now in the new normal? Do you have the right leadership framework in place to be able to support your leaders for now and in the future?

And understanding where you are on your leadership journey is important, so are you…

- An organisation who has laid the foundation for leadership but now want to build leadership capability, leadership pipeline and future-proof your leaders?

- An organisation that that has pockets of command-and-control style leadership looking to break dysfunctional and hierarchical behaviours?

- Looking for new ways to think about leadership during these times of uncertainty and change, that bring survival or reinvention challenges in an ever more competitive and digital environment?

- Currently in the process of transforming HR to keep pace with the latest in agile and digital, looking to be part of the dawn of the next stage organisations whose leaders will shape the future?

What is very apparent with all the change going on in the world and the advances to come, is what brought you success in the past will not be guaranteed in the future. This is why it is so important to have a growth mindset and continually learn and refresh your leadership and work skills. The onset of the fourth industrial revolution is upon us, are **you** ready for the future?

The best way to predict the future is to create it…

A Quick Reminder

- The Semmelweis Effect means it can be very difficult to move beyond pre-existing norms and beliefs about leadership.

- We now live in a world where the rate of learning is not keeping up with technological change which requires new ways of thinking about leadership.

- In a recent Gallup study, it is claimed that 50% of employees are not engaged and 1 in 2 leavers leave because of their manager.

- This is because leaders lack empathy, or the organisation or manager does not provide flexibility and meet employee desires.

- Although there are some generational differences in the workforce, today's leaders should be able to flex and adapt leadership styles to the needs of each individual.

- There is a leadership spectrum from command-and-control styles to empowering leadership to treating individuals as leaders.

- Employees want meaning and purpose in what they do and the Ikigai framework is a great way to understand this.

- The requirements and expectations of a leader have definitely changed, the landscape has changed as we face the burning platform that the pandemic has created.

To Do:

- *Where is your leadership or organisations leadership on the leadership spectrum?*

- *Where is your organisation on its leadership journey? Are you and your organisation ready for the future?*

The Big Idea

- Employees want to be treated like leaders, so leaders should develop the mindset that their people are leaders. As we move into the future, this should be to create and develop leaders who have an understanding and accountability to make a difference in the organisation and in the world.

A Leadership Lesson from the Wolf Pack

"When the snows fall and the white winds blow, the lone wolf dies, but the pack survives."- Ed Stark, character in 'Game of Thrones'

Wolves teach us many lessons, but none so more as to the importance of sticking together and collaborating, even in the harshest of conditions.

Wolves travel in packs that have a hierarchical structure. Wolves also have a complex communication system which makes the pack effective when working together. The alpha male and female are the leaders of the pack, and responsibilities such as protecting the pack or hunting for the rest. Each wolf knows his or her place and sticks to his or her responsibilities. This helps the wolfpack function cohesively.

A pack of wolves has a much greater chance of bringing down a sizable kill than a lone wolf and they understand this and use it to their advantage. Wolves don't just hunt together; they play together too. Wolves know that the team that plays together, stays together.

There is so much we can learn from wolves about the importance of teamwork, collaboration and trust, which is especially important when it comes to leadership and building successful teams in the workplace.

Habitat: Wolves are found in North America, Europe, Asia, and North Africa. They tend to live in the remote wilderness, though red wolves prefer to live in swamps, coastal prairies and forests.

Scientists have estimated that around 200,000 to 250,000 wolves are left in the world.

Wolves are a lesser endangered species on the Earth

2

Time Travel to the Past

Where have we been?

An understanding of our leadership conditioning

> *"There is nothing impossible to him who will try."*
> — Alexander the Great, Greek military general

In 1961, the Milgram Experiment at Yale University literally shocked people, not only those who took part in the experiment but all those who heard about it. Volunteers observed a person take a test and if the answer was incorrect, they had to administer an electric shock. Most of the volunteers gave electric shocks when ordered to, by the person in control of the experiment. The person in control was in fact an actor but no-one actually received an electric shock – the whole experiment was a set-up to see how people would follow instruction. What was frightening, is once ordered to give the electric shocks, most volunteers did so, some to almost fatal levels.

Many of us have heard of this experiment, which reinforces the fact that most people will follow orders within reason, especially when being paid to do so, and when they see or know other people have carried out the same behaviour.

Another experiment was conducted with a group of people waiting at a doctor's surgery, and every time a buzzer sounded people would stand. Most people in the room had been given the brief to stand up every time they heard it. Those that hadn't very quickly conformed and every time they heard the buzzer they too stood up.

Eventually each person who had been given the brief was taken out of the room and new people who came in conformed to the same behaviour. Eventually, no-one in the room knew why they were standing up for the buzzer, yet everyone in the room continued to stand!

This is so powerful when we think about leadership and how when we lead by example, or bring a few first followers onside, the impact on the rest of the group is so profound. Conditioning and conformity play such a massive part in workforce and organisational behaviour. Based on the above, it also reinforces that what has generally happened in the past becomes accepted as the norm and because of this, organisational conditioning will be an integral part of what people do without most people actually knowing the reason for it.

'We have always done it this way', becomes the motto embedded deeply in the subconscious of all employees and its impacts hold back growth and new ways of thinking. Therefore it is important when working in organisations we analyse the conditioning that might be holding us back; as in our own lives the same can be true of leadership. Imagine we were able to complete time travel and we could travel back through time to different epochs of leadership. What and who would we find that defined leadership for humankind and created that conditioning?

I imagine arriving back in the time of the Hunter-gatherers, watching them hunt across the savanna chasing down giants like buffalo but also being mindful of not being prey with sabre-tooth tigers also in the fray. Hunting in packs would have been essential to success.

Hunter-gatherers – what did leadership look like?

Hunter-gatherer culture is a type of subsistence lifestyle that relies on hunting and fishing animals and foraging for wild vegetation and other nutrients like honey and berries for food. Up until approx. 11,000-12,000 years ago, all humans practiced hunting-gathering.

Anthropologists have discovered evidence for the practice of hunter-gatherer culture by modern humans (Homo sapiens) and their distant ancestors, dating as far back as two million years. Before the emergence of hunter-gatherer cultures, earlier groups relied on the practice of scavenging animal remains that predators left behind.

Hunter-gatherers would have formed rather like wolf packs, with a hierarchical system that provided roles for all in the pack. Leadership normally would have been through a chronological system or probably the strongest or fittest person within the pack. At certain ages, women would have been revered so we cannot assume that men led the pack, and we cannot assume patriarchal rule.

Leadership probably depended upon the activities of the pack of tribe, and most anthropologists believe that hunter-gatherers did not have permanent leaders; instead, the person taking the initiative at any one time would depend on the task being performed. It was probably the greatest hunter who was the leader of the society. A leader who could hunt and feed the tribe would have been seen as most valuable and leadership would not have been hereditary. However, staying within family packs or tribes would have been the norm.

Like children left alone to play, it is likely though at times that leadership would have been decided by competition and vying for dominance would have been the norm in certain tribes. Those who learnt the ways of the hunter-gatherer and had rituals or traditions probably would have had clear lines of responsibility within the tribe. Like the wolf pack, hunter-gatherers would have known working as a team was far more powerful than going it alone.

It is also possible that the leader might have been the most knowledgeable person. As there was no way to capture knowledge, the person who could remember the most could possibly have been the ultimate leader or most revered. Perhaps like worker bees, ensuring the Queen Bee is well-looked after in the hive, it might have been the tribe serving the elder who had wisdom and knowledge that was all important for survival of the species.

What can we learn about leadership from hunter-gatherers?

Research into existing hunter-gatherers find that the common good is most important within the tribe. For example, the modern-day Hadzabe tribe of Tanzania embody the notion that "the servant-leader is servant first." They don't recognize any leaders or any one person as having more power or influence than others have.

Robert Greenleaf, the father of Servant-leadership, defined servant-leadership as, "The servant-leader is servant first. It begins with the natural feeling that one wants to serve. Then conscious choice brings one to aspire to lead. The best test is: do those served grow as persons; do they, while being served, become healthier, wiser, freer, more autonomous, more likely themselves to become servants?"

In South Africa there is a famous saying...

"Your pain is my pain, my wealth is your wealth, your salvation is my salvation."

The South African word, *ubuntu*, means that a person is a person because of or through their interaction with others. *Ubuntu* encompasses the ability to express mutuality, compassion, and a desire to build communities that are just and caring. *Ubuntu* is an idea that goes deep in African culture. This has been passed down through the generations and runs through to the servant-style leadership of Nelson Mandela.

It is this kind of modern day understanding that has come through generations of the past and what likely kept the collective tribe together back in hunter-gatherer times. There is so much we can learn from this today in the power struggles that rage across the world, the wars of religion, the in-fighting within society, terrorism and the breaking up of society and nations as we continue to argue over beliefs and opinions, instead of demonstrating love and compassion.

But maybe that is part of our hereditary journey - that we prefer being in small tribes, we prefer servant leadership for our own tribe rather than for those outside our pack. Maybe we are actually being true to our past. Either way we can still learn the important lesson that servant leadership teaches us, the impact this can have on modern leadership and motivating others.

The Agricultural Revolution – Agrarian Times

The Neolithic Revolution—also referred to as the Agricultural Revolution—is thought to have begun about 12,000 years ago. It coincided with the end of the last Ice Age, and it forever changed how humans live, eat, and interact, paving the way for modern civilization.

There were eight Neolithic crops: emmer wheat, einkorn wheat, peas, lentils, bitter vetch, hulled barley, chickpeas, and flax.

Population pressure was a factor in areas of the world that would have created the need to cultivate food. New technological advances of the time with enhanced irrigation methods meant the mass production of existing foods, and moving into the realms of experimentation with new foods. Over the generations, populations across the world moved from hunter-gathering to farming, and with each new generation the old ways became forgotten.

Humans will have farmed prior to this but never on the scale to mass produce fruit and vegetables to sell and feed the growing population. It still remains a mystery as to why cereal-farming became so dominant and why hunter-gatherers passed on their easier lifestyle in favour of the hardship of farming each day and farming a narrow range of crops and managing livestock. Perhaps it was sheer numbers and the need to settle, rather than continual roaming.

Farming for most families or clans would have been about self-sustainability and surplus food used for when weather impacted crops, but it was quickly learned that mass production of food could then lead to selling of crops to help make a living. Food could be traded at local markets and became the onset of the agricultural revolution. The growth of agriculture resulted in intensification, which had important consequences for social organization. Complex societies took the forms of larger agricultural villages, cities, city-states, and states, which shared many features. Specialized labour gave rise to distinct social classes, and a hierarchal system within society was formed.

If leadership was about self-sacrificing during hunter-gatherer times, then what did we learn about leadership during the agricultural revolution?

As society formed from family tribes to people settling in much larger groups, it developed to create hierarchical social structures. This led to the need for the organisation of distribution of food, water, and control of the local population. Over time, this led to state boundaries and rulers with the onset of royalty-based leadership where the King, Queen or Head of State had power. This power initially may have been wielded for good but over time, with Divine Right and ownership of power, came expectations of the people set by leadership, eventually to taxes and distribution of wealth agreed by the leader of the people/state. Leadership moved away from self-sacrificing to a self-centred model.

With this came politics and religion to create a different level of depth and understanding of leadership. From being the leader as head of state, to leader of an army, to a leader within society, to the leader within one's own house. The most significant change became that of male leadership through religion and male dominance as the head of royal families. It moved away from collaborative and self-sacrificing leadership of the hunter-gatherers to hierarchical systems and the leader being seen as having power over others. We understand from history that there were both fair leaders and those who were out-and-out tyrants. But what changed was a movement away from collaborative leadership to one of birth-right leadership and as a result, to coercive and hierarchical leadership.

Leadership from the Past

Let's explore a number of those leaders...

Boudica

Boudica's husband, Prasutagus, King of the Iceni tribe, met his death in 60 AD. She then became Leader and Queen of the tribe.

The Romans demanded her inheritance and lands after Prasutagus died, which she refused, so they set an example by arresting and brutally lashing her and raping her daughters. Boudica then led the Celtic rebellion against the Romans, uniting the local tribes and gaining revenge. Fearsome in battle, Boudica led by example by leading her troops. Sadly, she was eventually defeated in battle by a superior Roman army who strategically placed themselves on a hill gaining a huge advantage, Even though Boudica had superior numbers, she lost the battle and many great Celts died.

> *"It takes skill to win a battle, but brains to win a war."*
> — Amy I. Long,' The Untold Legend: The Warrior Queen'

What did we learn from Boudica's leadership?

The ability to unite people around a common goal, the courage to lead troops into battle and the strength to lead as a woman. What Boudica lacked was strategic leadership and understanding of battle to actually win the war. But she is a great example of leadership - people followed her because she was Queen but more importantly, because they believed in her cause.

Alexander the Great

Alexander the Great thought he was the son of a God, was educated by Aristotle and became a leader of the Macedonian Army at a young age.

Alexander had a vision of conquering the unknown world and he led his troops into battle. He overthrew the Persian empire, conquered Asia all the way to India, and laid the foundations for the Hellenistic world of territorial kingdoms.

Alexander was a man of integrity; after capturing Darius's wife and family he treated them with chivalrous respect and even after defeating Darius, who was the leader of the Persian Army, he sent his body to be buried in the royal tombs of Persepolis. Alexander learned well from Aristotle - not just philosophy but how to be a great leader.

"Through every generation of the human race there has been a constant war, a war with fear. Those who have the courage to conquer it are made free and those who are conquered by it are made to suffer until they have the courage to defeat it, or death takes them." — Alexander the Great

What did we learn from Alexander's leadership?

Aristotle had the ultimate self-belief because he believed he was the son of a God; he was able to sell his vision to his troops and they followed him with the same belief he had for his cause. What we also see from Alexander, was that he was a values-based leader, in how he demonstrated respect for his enemies. And it was why he was accepted and revered on his travels and still is to this day.

Genghis Khan

Genghis Khan experienced the murder of his father when he was only nine, and his own tribe was expelled. In his teens he was captured by rival clans and spent time as a slave before escaping. Despite this, he was able to bring together the local tribe into a massive army by 1206 with the Steppe Confederations under his banner.

While it's impossible to know for sure how many people perished during the Mongol conquests, many historians put the number at somewhere around 40 million.

Genghis led with coercive power and through fear and ensured no one could come back from defeat for revenge, hence why he killed all in his path. This was based on his own experience from his father's death, his fear of assassination meant he brought fear to others during his reign and left no prisoners.

"It is not sufficient that I succeed - all others must fail." – Genghis Khan, warrior and founder of the Mongol Empire

What can we learn from Genghis Khan's leadership?

Genghis Khan is the perfect example of coercive, command-and-control leadership who led his troops through fear. Whereas Alexander the Great created a vision that his troops were motivated by being 'towards' i.e. towards the vision, Genghis Khan created the opposite. It was fear that his troops were moving away from i.e. away from possible death if they didn't do as they were told. Khan was also highly adept at strategic warfare and able to conquer China which is no small feat in itself.

Jesus Christ

Everyone knows the story of Jesus. His leadership style was completely values-based and self-sacrificing, putting the needs of others first through love. Named the Son of God at the Council of Nicaea in 325AD, we may presume that his leadership was strategic being all-knowing but what we know from the stories is that Jesus's leadership was very much in the moment. So this gives us four very unique styles that enable us to see how leadership developed.

"A new command I give you: Love one another. As I have loved you, so you must love one another." – **(John 13:34)**

The Quadrant Model of Leadership

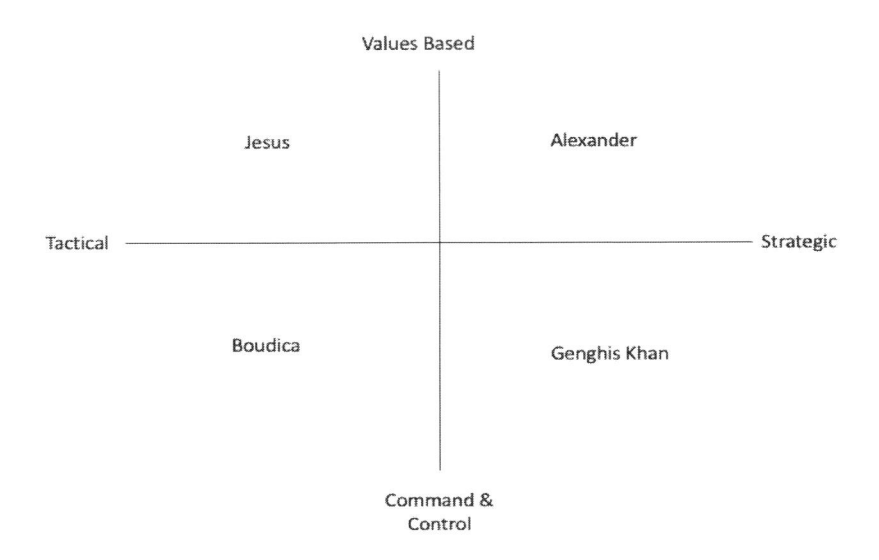

```
                    Values Based
                         |
         Jesus           |        Alexander
                         |
                         |
Tactical ────────────────┼──────────────── Strategic
                         |
                         |
         Boudica         |        Genghis Khan
                         |
                    Command &
                     Control
```

The Age of Exploration and Mercantile Era

The period from the early 15th century into the early 17th century, was the Age of Exploration, where European ships sailed the world searching for new trading routes and to create partnerships or 'civilise' the unknown world. The impact of exploration would permanently alter the world and transform geography, creating new trading routes, laying the foundation for the future. Explorers learned about new parts of the world, exploiting the people and precious commodities through coercive force or trading in goods. They brought back extensive knowledge, new foods, plants, animals and methods of navigation and mapping of the world to produce the first nautical maps.

Sadly, indigenous people were decimated or forced into the slave trade, pointing to completely selfish leadership and little care for the rights of the new people they had discovered.

The mindset of an explorer is interesting. Where most people stayed in their local area for most of their lives, some individuals have what is called the Explorer's Gene, with the incessant need to travel. Many who sailed in this age would have done so as a means to survive and pay their way when back home. But the real explorers - the captains and leaders who thrived on travelling to new destinations - would have had a thirst for finding new lands, learning new things about the world and new experiences. What we do know is that those who were under command of the captain of the ship were normally lead in a style of command-and-control. Each person on the ship would have had a role and expected to conduct that role on the captain's orders, whether they be soldiers, sailors, or crew. What we start to see though is new ways of thinking innovatively about ship design to travel long distances, and the strategic vision to conquer unknown lands and the possibilities within them.

We see this in Christopher Columbus, to Vasco da Gama, to Captain James Cook; all legendary in their travels into the unknown to find undiscovered lands and claim them for King or Queen and Country.

The War Generals – The Influence of Personality

Over the years there have been countless wars across the world; from battles with bow and arrow, sword, and shield, to bayonets and guns, to ships and airplanes - you name it, we have continued to wage war.

Our past record when to comes to peace overall is not very good and with limited resources in the future it has never been more important to build a sustainable future. Over-population and lack of water as the planet heats up may just drive the next world war at some stage but when we do look back as a species, we are warmongers.

Let's focus on two war generals from the Battle of Waterloo in 1815.

Napoleon Bonaparte had a massive impact on history; he was a brilliant leader and he laid the foundations for what France is today. He had an amazing military mind both as a tactician and strategist. He was fearless leading his troops on the battlefield, and at times he was a charismatic leader who was listened to by his people. What made Napoleon a great example of a leader was his ability to connect at every level, even getting down from his horse to help out in the trenches. He realised this set an example but also gave him a chance to find out what his troops were really thinking. Even though some consider him a tyrant, Napoleon demonstrated great respect to those around him and he understood the importance of attention and motivation. The devotion and loyalty he showed his soldiers was repaid in their faith in his cause, transforming his army into an incredible force. However, with Napoleon's genius came his flaws; he was over-ambitious, egotistical, egocentric, often unpredictable and irrational.

"A leader is a dealer in hope." – Napoleon Bonaparte, French military and political leader

Napoleon's nemesis at the Battle of Waterloo was the Duke of Wellington, who rose to prominence as a general during the Peninsular campaign of the Napoleonic Wars. He is regarded as one of the greatest defensive generals of all time and his tactics and strategy are still studied to this day. His character was far more stable than Napoleon's and he had the belief in his own judgement, with an inner confidence in his ability that made him the great military general he was. In complete contrast to Napoleon's passion, Wellington rarely showed emotion in public, and often appeared condescending to those less competent or less well-born than himself. He was known as the Iron Duke, as he was a consistent and strong leader. Although known as a defensive tactician, he also led many offensive strikes during battles and was very responsive to the needs of the battle to quickly adapt his tactics.

Both men were incredible generals with one passionate, warm, connected to his troops but unpredictable, and the other cold, consistent, adaptable, and responsive.

"The whole art of war consists of guessing at what is on the other side of the hill." – The Duke of Wellington, British military commander and twice Prime-Minster of the United Kingdom

So here we have the classic example of a people-leader and a task-leader. One who could connect and lead people inspirationally, and the other who was focused on the job at hand to provide strong and clear direction. Both were incredible generals but demonstrate the impact of personality on leadership and also differing leadership styles that we can learn from. Napoleon vision is proactive to conquer, and Wellington's is reactive and responsive to the oppressor at hand.

There are so many leaders in history that we could discuss but the general theme is the greatest leaders had strategic insight into leading and motivating their troops although their styles were different, and their personality impact their style.

What is noticeable is that strong directive leadership will get you results, but it is very important to take your troops with you and for them to know that you care. Otherwise, mutiny on the bounty or revolution awaits all leaders if human leadership is not practiced especially in the times we now live.

The Industrial Revolution

Going back in time to the Industrial Era, we would have usually seen coercive command- and-control leadership within the boss/worker relationship. Karl Marx called it the relationship between "the bourgeoisie", i.e. the people who control the means of production in a capitalist society, and "the proletariat" i.e. the members of the working class. The power of command-and-control remained in the hands of the bourgeoisie until the start of the Trade Unions who started to ask for workers' rights. As an organized movement, Trade Unionism originated in the 19th century in Great Britain then across Europe and America. Initial movements in the 18th century were crushed or prosecuted, but the labour movement gained momentum and received its legal foundation in the Trade-Union Act of 1871.

Trade Unions would gain power as each decade went on through the 20th century. Although workers' rights improved, when it came to leadership, command-and-control was still the main style of the times, but with bosses slowly starting to realise that leadership needed to change to keep up with the times…

"Leadership teachings of most of the twentieth century focused on directive, autocratic (or at least top-down) management. The boss was expected to know the answers, or at least what to do. He, (and it was usually a man for most of the period), would tell people what to do . . . and they did what they were told. Strict rules were in force and there were serious consequences for violating the social system.

In the spirit of McGregor's Theory X, it was assumed that most workers could not think for themselves and, therefore, needed a superior to direct their efforts. Sometimes the "leader" actually was superior in intellect, experience, skill, understanding, or longevity, but often the power came from the position itself. "I'm boss, so you must do what I tell you."" - Joyce L. Gioia, MBA, CSP, CMC.

As work evolved over the years, workers started to think more about their conditions and how they could manage their own work. So we started to see a move to a more democratic style of leadership in some organisations and factories, being the opposite to coercive power and more associated with McGregor's Theory Y. As Gioia goes on to mention, organisations and factories then decided to make all company decisions by committee. This collaborative and democratic approach laid the foundations for the changes of leadership to come.

The Onset of the Office

The 1970s and 80s saw the onset of the office and new dynamics coming into play as teams became the norm. The command-and-control leadership style moved to laisser-faire and more democratic styles but what was visible was transactional leadership.

I give you something - pay, benefits, car parking, a bonus - and you give me something in return. This worked initially because it was a new way to treat workers and kept workers in jobs until the end of their careers with the boss ultimately in control. But with changing times, workers no longer had a job for life so the way companies gained followership was to throw incentives and bigger bonuses and perks to tie its people down but also meant a shift in leadership was required. Over the years, unfair incentives and ones that were just not ethical have been replaced and seen the whole employee value proposition and the psychological contract redrawn. But this alone is not enough to keep employees motivated and inspired to retain top talent, leaders, and employees.

The discovery of emotional intelligence (EQ) brought new ways to think about leadership and an understanding that leaders with high EQ are better leaders than those with high IQ. EQ was a new wave of leadership, and the move to empowering people, listening to them and coaching them. The whole concept of leading people and an understanding of leadership versus management was essential if you wanted to be a successful leader. And the advent of the coaching revolution, along with the use of psychometrics were the spark to develop a leader's self-awareness, aligned to EQ.

The situational leadership model described the way a leader should use different styles dependent upon the situation, in simple terms along a spectrum from directive to coaching that we explored Chapter 1.

The Knowledge Era

With the onset of the Internet and Google-type search functions, we quickly realised that we no longer needed to remember everything or go find our hard-backed encyclopaedias. We could ask any question and Google had the answer. At the same time, this started to translate into leaders not needing to know everything. Although this has taken decades since the onset of the internet, the mindset of society has completely changed as any answer can be found very quickly online. This change in mindset slowly dripped into the understanding that a leader does not need to be all-knowing and in fact a team of people, other departments or subject matter experts can be asked and trusted to give the correct information.

This has been a massive leap from the controlling leader who needs to know everything, to the new trust that we find in corporate organisations of today. This, along with the introduction of emotional intelligence, situational and transformational leadership, is what more clearly defines what 'good' looks like for leadership now.

An excellent article by consulting firm Korn Ferry called *The Third Wave* prior to the pandemic explained the leadership shift is now moving to one of Agency, Authenticity and Agility. And we see amazing strategic and innovative leadership, especially in the big tech companies like Apple, Amazon, and Facebook to name a few, although it is a shame the same can't be said when it comes to our world and political leaders.

- Agency - leaders will require a sense of purpose in the work they do.
- Authenticity - leaders will be genuine and act with integrity in everything they do.
- Agility - leaders will be able to adapt to move with the uncertainty and change in the world.

This model still applies in the times we now live but it is worth mentioning the paper was pre-pandemic, which brings us up to date. This has been a quick trip back through history, only skimming the surface. And leadership now brings accepted new ways of working with hybrid and remote leadership all part of the new normal and current jigsaw most leaders are trying to solve.

So, when we look back to the past, Leadership has evolved to move away from hive- style leadership in hunter-gatherer times, to hierarchical command-and-control. This conditioning through the ages has meant that those in power have tended to exert coercive leadership upon others because they could. But what is noticeable is the impact of personality on leadership and how the importance of developing a leader's self-awareness is key to their success. By looking at the different leadership styles from leaders of the past, we can see similarities and differences that point to their values and skills as a leader.

What we have seen in the last 200 years is a greater understanding and exploration of what it means to be a good leader, how to lead and being a leader at every level in the workplace. New leaders need to understand what 'good' looks like or they quickly conform to out of date stereotypes of what it means to be a leader through command-and-control. Similar to the Milgram Experiment, leaders can easily become very dysfunctional if they do not understand what 'good' looks like. Hence the importance that organisations make their definition of leadership and leadership models very clear, so behaviours can be role-modelled.

Leadership has changed and it has evolved to the point of greater understanding of what it means to be a good leader.

However, the times we now live in due to exponential change means that leadership needs to make a step change so that leaders now create leaders. More importantly that they see their people as leaders in this new world of uncertainty and change.

A Quick Reminder

- It is most probable that hunter-gatherers used a style of hive leadership and collaboration

- Once farming became the main way of life, hierarchical structures developed

- With these hierarchical structures came the onset of command-and-control leadership through royal, fiefdom, religious, tribal, or family structures.

- There has always been command-and-control leadership through armies and controlling others such as slaves, however the onset of civilised society saw this become the normal leadership practice inherent in the civilised world.

- By looking at leaders from the past and their values or tactical or strategic approach, we are able to plot their leadership style on the Quadrant Leadership Model to gain insight into different leadership styles.

- Although command-and-control styles of leadership would have been predominant with the great explorers and their crew, the leader explorers demonstrated great strategic vision.

- As a species we have always been warmongers and fail to live in peace which means command-and-control leadership will always be prevalent.

- The Industrial Revolution and the onset of factories saw the embedding of command-and-control leadership deeper within society as the boss had complete control over the workers – the bourgeoise over the proletariat.

- Trade Unions fought for workers' rights and the balance of power was slowly re-addressed.

- The office revolution brought new ways of working through teams and with the understanding of the importance of EQ and situational leadership, a move away from transactional leadership started.

- The Internet enabled us to search for any answer, so we no longer needed to remember everything; this in turn paved the way for a move away from the 'All Knowing' Leader.

- We live in times that now call for Agency, Authenticity and Agility from our leaders, especially as we navigate the pandemic and new ways of working.

To Do:

- *What can you learn about leadership from the past?*
- *What leaders can you learn from in the past?*
- *Where do you fit on the Quadrant Leadership Model?*
- *Are you an emotionally intelligent leader?*
- *Are you an 'All Knowing' leader? Do you need to be?*
- *Do you demonstrate Agency, Authenticity and Agility?*
- *How can you learn from leaders in the past to help you move along the leadership spectrum?*

The Big Idea
Understanding the past provides a gateway to the future. If we can understand how we have negatively been impacted by coercive styles of leadership, we can embrace the need to move along the leadership spectrum into the future.

A Leadership Lesson from the Beehive

"If the bee disappears from the surface of the Earth, man would have no more than four years left to live." – Albert Einstein, theoretical physicist

Hive: a verb that means to move together as one, like a swarm of bees. Bees truly are brilliant team workers, and it is called a hive for a reason.

Bees use vibrations and pheromones to help pass complex messages.

As bees mature, they move through all the jobs in the hive before becoming food gatherers.

Bees make honey while the sun shines, they store the extra food when times are good as they know that there may be leaner times around the corner.

We tend to think of the 'Queen Bee' as the leader of the hive, sitting regally, whilst her workers bring home the nectar. In truth, the queen is the servant of the team, laying the eggs to ensure the future survival of the colony.

Habitat: Honeybees live in large family groups called colonies. A full-sized colony at the height of the growing season contains an average of 60,000 individual bees. Honeybees tended by beekeepers live in wood boxes called hives.

There are more than 20,000 distinct bee species around the world with two trillion estimated numbers.

Bees are a lesser endangered species.

3
Megatrends of the Future

What will we become?

An exploration into how the future will change

"Disneyland will never be completed. It will continue to grow as long as there is imagination left in the world." – Walt Disney, American entrepreneur and film producer

In 1923, Walt Disney, along with his brother Roy, created the Disney Brothers Cartoon Studio in Hollywood, California. The studio is now known as the Walt Disney Company, with a portfolio of incredible films and Disneyworld Parks across the world. Walt Disney had a vision for the future, and as a talented artist, from a young age he drew cartoons for publications. Walt was to go bankrupt before he eventually hit the big time and with the 1928 release of *Steamboat Willie,* the world was introduced to Mickey Mouse. The popularity of Mickey Mouse in short films, convinced Walt to create a feature film in 1934. This led to the creation of *Snow White and the Seven Dwarfs* which was a smash hit in 1937. The rest is history with film after film being a hit and theme parks opening across the world from 1955.

The Walt Disney Company now owns and operates ABC, ESPN, Pixar, Lucas Film and Marvel Studios. Disney transformed his ideas from his initial cartoons, into full feature films, to ultimately, having a team of Imagineers creating the Disney Theme Parks we now know today.

Walt Disney Imagineering is the creative engine that designs and builds all Disney theme parks, resorts, attractions, and cruise ships worldwide, and oversees the creative aspects of Disney games, merchandise product development, and publishing businesses.

Walt Disney said, "*All our dreams can come true, if we have the courage to pursue them.*" Disney had the drive and determination to see tasks through and was able to connect with those who worked for him. Disney was a salesman and understood the importance of vision, along with understanding the trends for the future in film with the opportunity it presented for his talents. His leadership characteristics of honesty, enthusiasm, creativity, persistence, and the ability to take others with him in pursuit of his vision and dreams, makes him a remarkable leader. An innovator who could see the opportunity to create a future based on imagination.

When we actually stop to think about his achievements, they are quite remarkable whether you are a Disney fan or not. But what it proves is that we are capable of creating our own future if we follow and learn from the success of those who have come before us and have been very successful. Because like Disney, people have been very successful before. In essence we can stand on the shoulders of giants. We explored the importance of understanding a history of leadership in the last chapter. Now fast forward, not to today, but to the future. How many of us are prepared for the exponential change the future holds? How many of us see the opportunity it presents? And how many of us can demonstrate the same type of entrepreneurial leadership that Disney demonstrated?

When we look to the future there are megatrends that we all need to be prepared for and understand if we are to future-proof ourselves for what is to come. We must consider how leadership needs to evolve in the face of these megatrends.

Megatrends are transformative and powerful forces that could change the global economy, business, and society. We have seen megatrends like the onset of the steam powered engine, electricity and more recently, the internet, that have in their time completely reshaped how we live our lives. Megatrends are generally long-term in nature but tend to have irreversible consequences for the world around us. But these longer-term megatrends can quickly bite us if we are not prepared for them, as with the Covid-19 pandemic. This was a megatrend that was expected by a few of us who were ready to respond to the outbreak, but for most of us it was very unexpected. Global megatrends are macroeconomic and geostrategic forces that are shaping our world and can provide great opportunity, while at the same time providing serious challenges to life on this planet.

The depth and complexity of megatrends will demand "whole of society" solutions and new ways of thinking if we are to successfully navigate the future. For most people, it is hard to see the future when their day-to-day life doesn't change too much. However, as we have all experienced through lockdown, these impacts are coming faster as the rate of change in the world is speeding up through technology and competitive forces that enhance but also challenge the world economies of today.

We must not fear the megatrends but it is important to understand what they are so we can be prepared, act with creativity and the right leadership to take us onwards into the future.

Understanding these megatrends gives us a vision of the future and enables us to fast forward to see the opportunities and challenges ahead, but also to consider how our leadership needs to evolve. As we move into the most transformational time in our history, can we adapt?

Let's explore the Megatrends and their potential impacts on the future:

Technology & Digitisation

Most organisations have experienced digital disruption in the last 10 years with advances in technology. Nokia, Kodak and Blockbuster are all examples of the losers, while Netflix, Amazon and Facebook are examples of those who have capitalised on digitisation. We have seen technical progress with further development of the internet, mobile applications and technologies using smart technology, artificial intelligence, and increasing globalisation. Over 125 billion internet-connected devices are expected to be in market by 2030, up from 17 billion in 2017. 10 years ago, you would never believe you would be watching your favourite film or series whilst commuting, or have the power to shop across the world, order your dinner from your phone and have more or less anything delivered to your door.

We have sport, films, TV, shopping, banking, games and much more all at our fingertips. Let me take you back to 1977, when *Grandstand* came out – this was a game of tennis which had two short vertical lines with a dot going across the screen! The rate of technological change has continued to speed up; in the 80s and most of the 90s we still made landline calls to meet our friends, the late 90s saw brick-sized mobile phones, then to the early 00s with text phones such as Nokia, to the onset of the Smart phone from 2007. Now we take this technology in our pockets for granted.

Technology trends emerging as a result of digitalisation, such as IoT (Internet of Things), AI (Artificial Intelligence), Robotics and next level process automation, data analytics through Big Data, Next Gen Computing, VR (Virtual Reality), and AR (Augmented Reality), with the advent of smart vehicles, cloud computing, streaming, smart grids, solar energy and the metaverse to name a few modern-day innovations. Breakthrough innovations in technology have become so much easier due to globalisation and digitisation. This has accelerated the adoption of new technologies around the world and technological growth has become exponential.

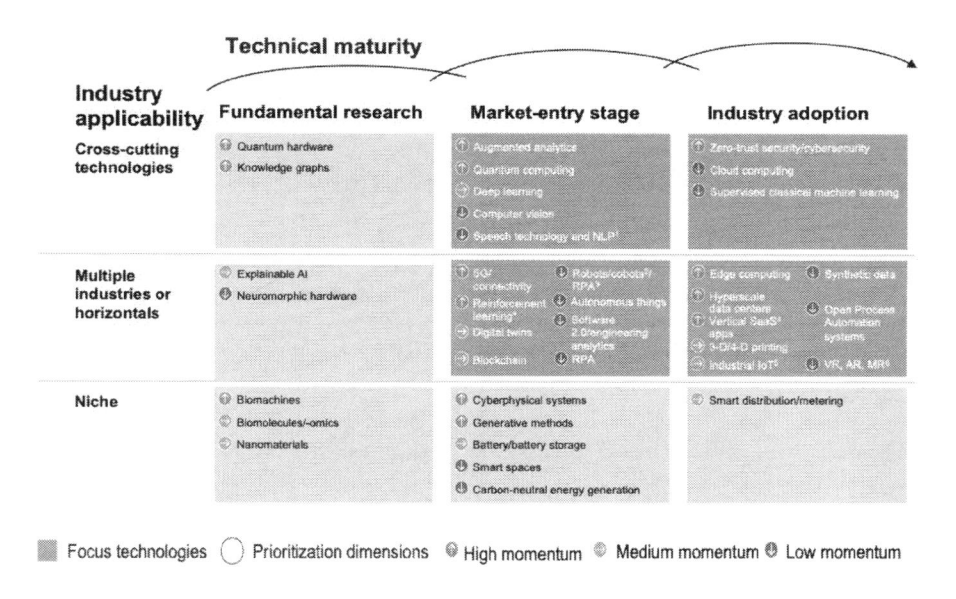

Industry applicability	Fundamental research	Market-entry stage	Industry adoption
Cross-cutting technologies	Quantum hardware; Knowledge graphs	Augmented analytics; Quantum computing; Deep learning; Computer vision; Speech technology and NLP	Zero-trust security/cybersecurity; Cloud computing; Supervised classical machine learning
Multiple industries or horizontals	Explainable AI; Neuromorphic hardware	5G connectivity; Reinforcement learning; Digital twins; Blockchain; Robotics/cobots/RPA; Autonomous things; Software 2.0/engineering analytics; RPA	Edge computing; Hyperscale data centers; Vertical SaaS apps; 3-D/4-D printing; Industrial IoT; Synthetic data; Open Process Automation systems; VR, AR, MR
Niche	Biomachines; Biomolecules/-omics; Nanomaterials	Cyberphysical systems; Generative methods; Battery/battery storage; Smart spaces; Carbon-neutral energy generation	Smart distribution/metering

Focus technologies ▪ Prioritization dimensions ○ High momentum Medium momentum Low momentum

https://www.mckinsey.com/~/media/McKinsey/Business%20Functions/McKinsey%20Digital/Our%20Insights/The%20top%20trends%20in%20tech%20final/Tech-Trends-Exec-Summary

New investment opportunities are opening up due to breakthroughs in artificial intelligence, nanotechnology, pharmaceuticals, and smart technology to see new players in the market, challenging the status quo. The internet, data analytics, cloud computing, smart devices and machine-learning capabilities will transform our world.

The image above shows more than 40 individual technologies by technical maturity, industry impact, and momentum provided by McKinsey & Co that separates technology into cross cutting technologies, multiple industries or horizontals and niche v technical maturity.

Rapid Urbanisation

In the 1950s, less than 30% of the world's population lived in cities. However, in the future mass migration will mean two-thirds of the world's population will live in cities by 2050, double the percentage from 1950. Cities are hubs for opportunity, open to diverse talent and places of innovation.

Large cities such as London, New York and Paris have invested in the right infrastructure to support the growing economy and to attract entrepreneurs and businesses into the city. As more people live in cities, the share of global growth is rising. In the last 10-15 years, China and other developing economies industrialised rapidly and large numbers of the population migrated to cities.

The growth in urban population will greatly increase in Asia and Africa and large-scale migrations from rural areas will power much of this growth. Large cities that offer the right infrastructure and opportunities attract the best talent, which leads to a boost to the economy through entrepreneurial success and innovation.

According to PwC...

"1.5 million people are added to the global urban population every week, placing huge demands on infrastructure, services, job creation, climate and environment. But this global urban transition presents significant opportunities too, with vast potential for emerging cities to act as powerful and inclusive development tools."

Traditional city models will be challenged by the rapid growth which requires the right infrastructure, technology, and business models to be a success. Technology, digitisation, and innovation provide the opportunity for new 'smart' cities to be developed to deal with rapid urbanisation but ongoing population growth will continue to add pressure on the mass migration which is already taking place. In the future, we will see the onset of mega cities and greater disparity of wealth.

Shifting Economic Power

There is a shifting of economic power to realign the world's economies with distribution of wealth and power. Emerging market economies today are predicted to represent 6 out of the 7 largest economies by 2050. The last 20 years has seen a shift from existing Western economies to developing economies aided by globalisation, shifting to Asia and China in particularly.

Two decades of unprecedented growth has lifted China's per capita GDP and it is expected that by 2050, China and India will have the largest economies.

The impact of this on a global scale will see a shift in the world; the Unites States has for a long time has been the main player and power across the world, so we will see a shift of economic power. This also threatens to destabilise world peace and has already begun with Russia testing the waters with Ukraine and U.S. sailing warships in Chinese waters.

The power of sanctions to uphold peace is only a tool when you have economic power to impact the opposing economy.

We will have to wait and see how, in the years to come, all these shifts will impact on the world and how they will start to play out as markets begin increasingly to open. From a positive perspective, global markets have never been more open with the opportunity to buy and sell goods due to globalisation.

We will continue to see ongoing globalisation with the ongoing integration and internationalisation of markets and the boundaries between different cultures more open and fluid.

Climate Change and Scarcity of Resources

We are all aware of the impacts of climate change and global warming on the planet, the impact that plastic is having on our oceans and carbon emissions on the greenhouse effect. Scarcity of resources and the impact of climate change is becoming one of the biggest global and economic concerns as our weather system becomes more unpredictable with each passing year.

This extreme weather and the potential rise in sea levels with Antarctica melting at an alarming rate, making hunting, farming, and fishing difficult and will have a serious impact on most of our coastal cities in the world. The ever-growing population creates a rising demand for food, materials and resources which continues to place great stress on our planet. The demand for energy will increase by as much as 50% by 2030 alone as the population grows.

"Prior to the Industrial Revolution, emissions were very low. Growth in emissions was still relatively slow until the mid-20th century. In 1950 the world emitted 6 billion tonnes of CO2. By 1990 this had almost quadrupled, reaching more than 22 billion tonnes. Emissions have continued to grow rapidly; we now emit over 34 billion tonnes each year." – Hannah Ritchie & Max Roser, Our World in Data.

Governments around the world are now investing in energy efficiency and renewable energy but there is still a long way to go to make an impact on climate change. Whether we can turn the tide before it has detrimental effects on our planet only time will tell.

"There is no going back - no matter what we do now, it's too late to avoid climate change and the poorest, the most vulnerable, those with the least security, are now certain to suffer." – Sir David Attenborough, broadcaster and naturalist

Demographics and Social Change

We are already seeing the demographic change through longer lifespans, and we are in the midst of better education on modern lifestyles which is changing our consumer habits, medicines and health.

The growing and aging populations of the world will impact jobs, immigration, different generational expectations, skills, and access to resources. There is a forecasted 45% increase in the 60+ population worldwide by 2030. Technology and automation will mean the workforce of tomorrow need to develop more advanced skills.

In the UK alone, we are now seeing an increase in those studying at university with graduate job applications increased by 41% in 2021. The future will mean increased competition for roles and a widening of talent pool. Due to the pandemic, there are now new ways of working in what has been described as the new normal.

This is the adaptation to remote and hybrid ways of working, along with the concept of smart working where possible.

Smart working being that you can work from anywhere in the world. And although we will see rapid urbanisation, we will also see some people move out of the city because they can work anywhere.

And as population continues to grow at an exponential rate, there is always the chance that we will face another pandemic, especially as climate change impacts our way of life, forcing more and more people into the cities. It is not so much the numbers but more the impact a future pandemic will have on megacities and people conglomerates across the globe.

There are already social impacts from lockdown and people are more adverse now to now socialising. With the launch of the multiverse, we will potentially have an even greater reason to stay at home. The multiverse will be able to provide all social interaction from the comfort of our own home via virtual and augmented reality.

The experience of meeting people will feel almost as real as meeting them in person. Imagine being sat around your kitchen table talking to the holograms of your friends and family, instead of talking over the phone or on FaceTime.

These changes will impact the way we live our lives with a new type of society, Society 5.0. Society 5.0 was originally proposed as a future society that Japan should aspire to, which now resonates with the current times. Society 5.0 is:

"A human-centred society that balances economic advancement with the resolution of social problems by a system that highly integrates cyberspace and physical space."

It follows the hunting society (Society 1.0), agricultural society (Society 2.0), industrial society (Society 3.0), and information society (Society 4.0).

The workplace of the future might not be hybrid or remote but multi-versed, as new ways of thinking about work are ahead of us on the horizon. With this brings social change across the globe.

The challenges we will face due to these megatrends.

As mentioned in the Introduction, the Four Riders of the Apocalypse are intertwined with the megatrends we now face, and those megatrends are either part the problem or part the solution. Climate change is a megatrend but also one of the Riders if we don't correct our course in time to save the planet. World war on the other hand could be caused by these megatrends but also could be due to egotistical leadership. Breakthrough innovations will be essential if we are to survive and thrive in the future, as well as a coming together and leadership diplomacy.

What will we become in the future?

What does the future hold when we hold in our hands the tools to change who we are biologically, genetically, and technically?

We are in the midst of intelligent design when it comes to the human race and our future. The question for the future will be: is the survival of homo sapiens possible when we hold the power to genetically change and upgrade our race?

Will we become 'homo deus' as Yuval Noah Harari describes in his brilliant book, *Homo Deus: A Brief History of Tomorrow*.

Biological Design

Our scientists re-engineer our genetics to remove genetic defaults, so we become Friedrich Nietzsche's 'Superman'. Do we then over time with each new birth only allow for genetically perfect babies to be born?

Do we eradicate homo sapiens in the same way that homo sapiens destroyed the Neanderthals, or will we interbreed and have three races: homo sapiens, 'homo deus' and hybrids, the latter the mixed race of the two? This would be all concocted in the laboratory with a programme of breeding of the species. Perhaps 'homo deus' will be known for their pedigree status, just as we label dogs - although I much doubt they will be for sale! - but never say never in the future. And in the search for this 'homo deus' perfection, do we then lose our soul? Will it be ethically possible, or will genetically modified humans be illegal? What makes us human at the end of the day is that we make mistakes… after all, we are human!

Perhaps in the future you will be able to go through genetic enhancement programmes to improve size, strength, intelligence, stamina and so on, but it will come at a price. There will be an Amazon shopping platform for genetic enhancements and it will be so expensive only the few will be able to live like Gods.

Will we end up creating our upgraded race and they in turn persecute us, abducting us then creating concentration camps? And just like in Mary Shelley's *Frankenstein*, the monsters we create will become obsessed with our annihilation. The annihilation of mere mortals by the superior race.

For those who are open to new theories of existence, there is more scientific evidence for the Ancient Alien theory than there is for the existence of God. Part of this theory is that although we may have evolved from apes, the genetic leap we made as a species was given to us via the helping hand of extra-terrestrials, through genetic modification.

In fact, the story of the Anunnaki in Sumerian legend, explains that man was enhanced to serve in the retraction of gold from the planet and we were upgraded to become intelligent slaves to the Anunnaki.

Perhaps only a myth but are we about to take the same course of action in genetically playing God with our own race and species?

Cyborg Design

We have already become part-cyborg with arm, hand, leg, and hearing replacements. But will the future be a shopping window of cybernetic parts where you can choose enhanced parts or add-ons to your body - three legs instead of two, four arms, bionic parts and so on? Does becoming the tentacled Doctor Ock from *Spiderman* or the Hindu god Kali seem so unbelievable? This may sound ridiculous but when you think about tattoos and body piercing and what people are currently willing to do to their bodies, this may end up being a choice. In ancient times, heads of young children and adults were bound with the Huns of Asia, the Mayans of Peru, the Chinookan Indians of the Americas and the Mangbetu of Africa as examples, to give their heads a prolongated look aligned to their Gods of the time or for status.

And in the future, there will be brain enhancements, such as the ability to plug straight into the brain to improve intelligence and skills, similar to Neo in *The Matrix* films when his Kung Fu ability is added. Once again, this may seem far-fetched, but the US army is experimenting with such a trial to enhance their troops cognitive and physical abilities. It has invested millions of funding for a programme to develop a 'brain chip' allowing humans to simply plug into a computer and to research the possibility of upgrading human capability and to give soldiers super-senses. DARPA officials have said the goal is 'developing an implantable system able to provide precision communication between the brain and the digital world.'

In the times we currently live, being part-cyborg is due to an accident or replacement of parts.

However, the future will create a new dimension as to what it means to be perhaps not completely human, but cyborg, especially when we consider the next type of intelligent design.

In-Organic Design

Whether this becomes an end-of-life option and choice or the freedom to choose a life within the matrix of the multiverse, we will find out in the future. There could be the possibility to upload your brain to the multiverse, or to a robot to prolong your life. What if being a cyborg actually meant that the only part of you that was human was your brain, and even that perhaps was uploaded to a key fob and inserted within a mechanical body?

Once downloaded, the brain 'recording' could be inserted into a human body grown from human embryo somehow kept alive, waiting for insertion, so that you could take control of a completely new body and shed the old one. Once again far-fetched, but could mind-loading be possible in the future?

As Wikipedia explains, "Substantial mainstream research is being conducted in animal brain mapping and simulation, development of faster supercomputers, virtual reality, brain–computer interfaces, connectomics, and information extraction from dynamically functioning brains.... Many of the tools and ideas needed to achieve mind uploading already exist or are currently under active development; however, others are, as yet, very speculative, but still in the realm of engineering possibility."

Some might feel that human life might not be for them, so will have the option to upload into what they may see as a more ideal world in the multiverse. Obviously, they will live for as long as the multiverse exists and will just have to hope the game doesn't get reset, the plug doesn't get pulled to early, literally, or there is a glitch in the system! Then again, cloud computing would keep you backed up!

What is fascinating, is that it has never been more important to understand what it means to be human and there will be some real and difficult ethical, political, philosophical challenges to work through, before any of the above will be agreed and approved. The same will be true when to comes to AI, as the argument rages as to whether AI, once fully realised, will be a good thing for humanity or a danger. Think *The Terminator* films starring Arnold Schwarzenegger, with the artificial intelligence defence network known as 'Skynet', created by Cyberdyne Systems, which becomes self-aware and triggers a global nuclear war in order to exterminate the human species. It is not difficult to quickly understand what the dangers could be if AI was left to make its own assumptions about the human race.

So where are we now, compared to the future?

We are now on the cusp of the Fourth Industrial Revolution, which is a way of describing the blurring of lines between the physical, biological, and digital worlds. It is the coming together of advances on the Internet of Things (IoT) which fuels artificial intelligence (AI), which in turn fuels robotics, quantum computing, Big Data and 3D printing and genetic engineering, amongst other technologies.

We are seeing a move from the initial digitalisation of the last 20 years to one of connectedness through smart technology, innovation, and the multiverse, along with other platforms that will now bring us together in new ways. New possibilities lie ahead and anything that cannot be digitised or automated will become valuable due to the nature of human capability required. Human-only traits such as creativity, imagination, intuition, and ethics will be where our opportunity lies and what will set us apart from the technology happening all around us.

The future that has been in our imaginings is now here.

Will your organisation make the most of these trends to pursue new heights of rapid innovation, improved performance, and significant achievement?

Walt Disney dared to dream and create an escape for us all with the Disney films, adventures, characters, and worlds, in effect a multiverse we have all been part of, but only from an objective perspective. We have never been fully immersed in the Disney Universe, but how long before we will be part of that universe and are able to create our own Disney characters to become 'Disney-versed'? Jeff Bezos, Elon Musk, Mark Zuckerberg and Bill Gates are the current trailblazers, but it makes you think: if Walt Disney came back to life in the times we now live, would he see opportunity to build an empire, or would he be concerned for the future survival of the human race?

The future is changing everyday...and Leaders will need to think differently to solve the problems it presents. Are you ready for the future?

A Quick Reminder

- Walt Disney was able to shape the future through vision, imagination and persistence to create the Disney Universe.

- The Megatrends of Technology & Digitisation, Climate Change & Scarcity of Resources, Rapid Urbanisation, Shifting Economic Power and Demographics and Social Change will shape the future.

- The Four Riders of the Apocalypse - Pandemic, Climate Change, Scarcity, War & Terrorism - are intertwined with the megatrends, and it will take breakthrough innovation and new levels of human thinking to ensure the survival of the human race in the future.

- The human species will possibly evolve in the future into three species: homo sapiens, homo deus, and hybrids, with cyborgs and possibly robotic synthetic human life as new ground-breaking genetic engineering and scientific breakthroughs are possible.

- The Fourth Industrial revolution is one of connectedness made possible by the Internet of Things (IoT), artificial intelligence (AI), robotics, quantum computing, Big Data, 3D printing, genetic engineering, and intelligent design, amongst other technologies.

- Human only traits such as creativity, imagination, intuition, and ethics will be where our opportunity lies and what will set us apart from the technology happening all around us.

- Leadership will need to keep up with the rate and pace of change, needing to adapt to new ways of being in the multiverse of opportunity and new ways of communicating and leading.

To Do:

- *Do you have a plan for the future?*
- *Are you up to date with future thinking in readiness for the changes to come?*
- *Are you considering how to use new technologies in what you do?*
- *Is your business strategy future-focused?*
- *How are you keeping your thinking and skills up to date in readiness for the future?*
- *As a leader, what are the implications for you in the future?*
- *How are you developing both yours and your leaders' creativity, imagination, intuition and ethics to ensure you stay ahead of technological change?*
- *Are you future-proofing your leaders?*

The Big Idea

Megatrends will massively impact the future, with ongoing changing challenges and opportunities – only human-only traits such as creativity, imagination, intuition and ethics will set us apart.

"You want to have a future where you're expecting things to be better, not one where you're expecting things to be worse." – Elon Musk, entrepreneur and founder of Space X and Tesla

A Leadership Lesson from the Eagles

"An eagle uses the negativity of a storm to fly even higher" – Eric Thomas, American motivational speaker and minister

Eagles are majestic birds, and they are admired as living symbols of power, transcendence, and freedom.

The first leadership lesson an Eagle can provide is they can scan for prey over 2 miles away, with amazing vision and focus on the task at hand. An Eagle's vision is essential for its survival and just as we have been exploring the future in the above pages, a leader's vision is just as important for their effectiveness.

Eagles are not afraid of an obstacle and love the storm, using it to their advantage. They are courageous and daring in their pursuit of prey as should a leader be when chasing their goals.

But obviously for a good cause, as Eagles mate for life. The prey they catch will be shared with their young and mate, so too should leaders transcend the need for power to provide servant leadership for their people.

Eagles are continually scanning the horizon for opportunity. In the world we now live it is so important that leaders keep their thinking and skills up to date, so they can move with confidence into the future.

Habitat: Most eagle species prefer building their nests on high cliffs and in tall trees near water bodies like streams, lakes, and rivers.

Scientists estimate there are now more than 24,000 in the wild.

Eagles are no longer on the endangered list due to effective conservation.

4
Redefining Leadership

Human-Centred Leadership

Developing the leaders the world now wants to see.

"Leadership is not about rank or title: it is a choice. It's a choice to provide care and protection for those of whom we are responsible." – Simon Sinek, British-American author and inspirational speaker

The 'Illumination Experiment" was conducted between 1924 and 1927 and was sponsored by the National Research Council in the USA. The Council conducted the experiment to identify if there was a relationship between productivity and the working environment, such as the level of lighting in a factory. The lighting was changed and even the smallest of changes saw an uplift in performance. In fact, any change in the lighting saw an uplift in productivity even if lesser quality lighting was provided. However, the gain in performance slowly diminished as the attention faded. The results achieved had been determined by the special attention of the group of people to the experiment itself. It was their awareness of the experiment and the attention in itself that provided the impetus to increase performance.

Inspired by this, experiments were conducted at this particular factory over the next eight years by Elton Mayo from 1928-1932, with a group of five women. They changed their environment continuously, with the initial findings supporting the illumination experiment. Jonathan Freedman (1981) summarizes the results of the next round of experiments as follows:

"Regardless of the conditions, whether there were more or fewer rest periods, longer or shorter workdays...the women worked harder and more efficiently."

Analysis of the findings by Henry Landsberger (1958) led to the term the "Hawthorne effect" which describes the increase in performance of individuals who are noticed, watched, and paid attention to by researchers or supervisors.

When you think about it, in general most people are motivated by **special attention.**

If you provide your partner or children with special attention, you will get a positive response – the same occurs when you lead people. When you provide special attention in the workplace it will lead to increased motivation and performance. In fact, one of the secrets behind motivating people is **special attention**. However, as that attention becomes the norm, it is no longer special attention, so the effect wears off. A tip for anyone struggling in a relationship is to take a look at what you currently do and start to think about how you can give special attention to the person you are with.

The father who spends too much time watching sport on TV or who stops to play hide and seek with his young children will notice the immediate impact; the wife who is busy working from home who takes time to read with her kids, the leader who instead of just buying a bottle of wine, gives a gift to celebrate an employee's success based on their interests. The difference that special attention provides is remarkable. If you want to be a great leader, have a special attention plan for your people and watch the results you can get by being considerate, kind, and thoughtful.

Why is this so important?

Because Leadership has never more needed leaders who know how to motivate and support their people. And special attention is a key strategy in a leader's toolkit for success. There has never been a more important time to develop leaders to be able to cope with the demands of uncertainty, change, and the ambiguity we all now face in the world of work. There is a moral obligation to ensure that leadership means something within organisations, and it is commendable to developing the leaders the world now wants to see.

Over the course of history as we have explored over the past few chapters, leadership has developed mostly based on leadership styles and leaders being in a position of power. But over the last 50 years, it has changed significantly, with new thinking and ideas about how to develop leaders, along with those theories on leadership we discussed at the start of this book. The world is now changing at an exponential rate, with the pandemic causing chaos and what once brought leaders success can no longer be guaranteed in the future. There will be continued disruption and ongoing change with technological advances, increased employee expectations, and ongoing impacts from the pandemic, leading to far greater demands on leaders than before. The impacts of those megatrends we discussed will massively shape our future and impact how leaders need to reframe their leadership for the future.

This means organisations needing to take a step back, to rethink ways of working and what leadership means, and to ensure they have leaders who can create the culture they desire, along with developing their people to meet the demands of now and the future. With the ongoing change and uncertainty, it has never been more important to analyse the role leaders play in organisations, employee engagement and how they impact organisational culture and profitability.

Ensuring leadership is defined and the right leadership architecture is in place has never been more important as we prepare for the future. A touch of special attention to the process of thinking about leadership is required.

Redefining Leadership

Where do we find ourselves right now? Most businesses and organisations fear for their survival, whereas in contrast some organisations are thriving taking up the opportunity the pandemic has created for them, whilst a few will remain operational with little or no impact. However, the world has changed, and this presents a plethora of conundrums that leaders have not had to face before. Moving from a living mindset to a survival mindset during a pandemic is a situation not seen for most of us in our lifetime. Moving from a living to a survival mindset means moving from a state of autopilot to one where the brain is doing over-time, meaning more stress and pressure on the nation's mental health.

Leadership is now being challenged not just to redefine its 'why' but its 'what, how, where, which and for whom'. Remote leadership and new ways of working in a radical new business landscape yet to be discovered will ensure leadership itself will evolve to new ways of thinking about leadership.

"Leaders create culture. Culture drives behaviour. Behaviour produces results."

– Edgar Schein, Professor and expert in Organisational Development

The challenge of maintaining or enhancing employee engagement during times of change, disruption and uncertainty, is one most, if not all, organisations now face with pandemic impacts and exponential change. Leaders will create your culture and they will also be the biggest impact on your employee engagement. If leaders are not provided with the guidance and understanding of how to lead, how to be a leader and what leadership means, then they can make simple mistakes and demonstrate dysfunctional behaviours. This will come from a poor understanding of how to lead or the mental model of experience that has come from observed leadership and management.

This mental model could be from a good example of a leader who demonstrated great leadership behaviour or if it could come from a dysfunctional manager; either way it is then mirrored and copied as acceptable behaviour. There is a fundamental gap in knowledge of what 'good' looks like if people copy the behaviours of a bad manager and sadly, they will not know any different. This can lead to micromanagement styles, or the demonstration of undesirable behaviours through coercive misuse of power or conforming to organisational conditioning. Bad management and poor leadership habits that have formed across an organisation are very common. Ever know someone get promoted because they are good at what they do but they are not so good when it comes to management and leadership?

The impact of dysfunctional leadership therefore will then be negative when it comes to the overall employment engagement of the organisation. In a study in 2019 completed by human resources management and software services company ADP of 10,000+ professionals, 23% said bad management was a drain on productivity and 1 in 2 according to Gallup leave their job because of their manager.

This emphasises not only the importance of leadership and management when it comes to creating culture, but also the need to ensure the right thought leadership, assessment and solutions are in place, so leaders fully understand what is expected of them. This is especially important in times of change and disruption, when a leader feels they are in new situations they have never faced before.

Research completed by the Global Leadership Forecast has shown that only about 14% of companies feel they have a strong bench, with digital transformation and disruption having a profound effect on leadership at every level.

As part of their research, Global Leadership Forecast found that three cultural shifts are needed the most in responding to disruption:

1. Inform decisions through data and analytics

2. Integrate multiple and diverse perspectives to drive change

3. Embrace failure in pursuit of innovation

And that too many organisations are taking a "do it yourself" approach to leadership development, but leaders need personalised experiences along with the opportunity to learn from internal and external mentors. Development needs to be experiential and immersive. The bottom line is there is more to developing leaders than providing a range of solutions and then expecting behavioural change. Hence why your leadership development strategy should be thought-through, responsive and aligned clearly to your business strategy and the changing world.

Leaders need to be developed earlier and understand what good looks like through well thought through leadership behaviours or model.

This defining of leadership provides the framework for leaders to be successful, to have a choice in how they develop and also have content to engage and inspire them to be effective leaders. Is your leadership development strategy as effective as it could be?

In March 2020 NeuroLeadership Institute (NLI) conducted structured interviews with 20 HR and talent leaders, as well as a survey of 568 business and HR leaders across various organisations and industries. They found that most leadership models tend to be long, convoluted, and difficult to remember, often consisting of dozens of complex and contradictory behaviours. Since they are not clear or memorable, they fail to successfully guide behaviour in critical leadership situations. NLI Research showed that only 38% of individuals take action on their models once or twice a week and that 44% of companies have models with more than 20 behaviours! This may explain why only 17% of leaders find their models easy to remember and only 27% of individuals consider their leadership model meaningful!

If your pain points or burning platform is to shift behaviours and remove organisational conditioning, then the first step should be to redefine what leadership means for your organisation and make it simple for your leaders to understand. The most effective models of leadership tend to have four/five key leadership behaviours or success factors. Make it simple and it will stick and can then be embedded through your Leadership Strategy.

Values-Based Leadership

It is also critical to focus on key behaviours that will enable leaders to be there for their teams in their time of need.

The balance between being human and still maintaining performance has never been greater. The need for calm, clear communication, and optimism in the face of adversity. The need to demonstrate whether they actually care and there is trust in the relationship with each individual in their team. And if right now, your organisation is moving from a living mindset to one of survival, you need strong leadership to see you through the change and disruption. But then for all organisations with new ways of working, it has never been more important to redefine what leadership means.

When we consider the change and disruption in the world right now, the type of leader required is one who offers humility, compassion and empathy. Leaders who will support their people like leaders in their own right through human connection. Leaders who lead with the responsibility of role-modelling company values and acting with respect, integrity and transparency.

From an ethical and moral perspective, we are all now demanding leadership to be value-based and for leaders to lead; leaders who lead with integrity, purpose and meaning for the best interests of humankind. This is easier said than done when we live in a world of mixed agendas and cross-purpose objectives, but the most successful leaders right now demonstrate the soft skills to connect, support and lead with compassion.

They are leaders for good.

Having values that individuals and leaders can see, understanding that there are trademark behaviours that can be lived and breathed, are essential for leadership success within organisations. Many organisations have this, but the truly successful ones have leaders who **role-model and live** the values and behaviours. They are believed and embedded throughout the organisation.

Leaders may have their own style and there will be debates about which leadership style model is best, but the starting point should be leaders understanding the values of the organisation and what the business stands for, along with the importance of values-based leadership for the organisation especially now in the times we live. But those values now need to translate in the world where a new kind of normal exists, where expectations and working practice are changing. The new normal is becoming normal and the mind shift change already happened in the pandemic age.

There have been some amazing strategic and innovative leadership over the years especially in the big tech companies such as Apple, Amazon, and Facebook to name a few. But when we look at leadership from an ethical perspective, have we have gone backwards in time? Or are we now being catapulted into the future where human connection becomes valued and expected in the age and onset of AI. That future is now. When big companies avoid paying taxes that normal everyday people pay, is this an organisational and leadership example of values-based leadership and ethical ownership? This is the fundamental problem between ethical values-based leadership and the importance of shareholder value and profit margins.

It is very similar to the age-old debate of balancing 'What' goals with the importance of 'How' behaviours during the performance management process. Most organisations are moving away from traditional performance management processes but the point of the 'How' behaviours being as important as the 'What' goals was always lost in translation.

All of this is nothing new. We know the Ancient Greeks provided examples for the importance of values-based and ethical leadership very clearly in their philosophy.

And Confucius's moral system was based upon empathy and understanding others, rather than divinely ordained rules. Yet in a modern world that is task and goal-focused, will we indefinitely now see the return of human beings valuing the importance of being human?

There are lots of questions for us based on what we can control... do your people know and understand the company values, then live and breathe them? Do they understand the importance of them in the times we now live?

Can you see the opportunity to reframe your organisation to create values-based leadership? Will empathy and compassion be valued? If you want to build employee engagement there are a number of factors that influence engagement levels such as the psychological contract an employee has with their employer, but it is of critical importance that your leadership and leaders are seen as credible, inspiring, caring, and understanding. In effect, that your leaders care, can be trusted and are committed to developing and supporting their people in these times.

A manager or leader who does what they say they are going to do, who is values and principles based, and who acts like a role model, has a massive impact on the engagement and culture of the organisation.

In a study by McKinsey & Co, (Global survey: War on Talent), 89% of employees were satisfied when the company delivers great leaders who are inspirational, supportive, empowering and focused on development.

In a time where individuals, leaders and organisations can do more to help and support others, their colleagues, and those who are well less off in the world, during this pandemic, it is now surely time for leaders for good on all levels and to showcase the type of leader the world now wants to see?

Defining What Good Looks Like

When I am asked how leaders should lead, the answer is simple…

Based on how leadership is defined for the organisation, aligned to the business strategy and the appropriate leadership architecture in place. As per Schein (1990), as mentioned above, who defines culture as a set of different values and behaviours that may be considered to be a guide to success.

How do leaders understand what they should do?

By understanding what good looks like when it comes to leadership for the organisation. The fact is no-one in this pandemic age is a completely natural leader.

There may be people who are more natural at certain tasks, or more dominant personalities who can take control, but actually understanding leadership and how to lead when people want to be empowered, given autonomy, and be trusted whilst balancing that with the organisation's agenda and needs, is no easy task.

Especially as the landscape of work is changing every day in this age of uncertainty and change.

New leaders do not naturally know how to lead unless they have learnt good practice from a prior manager, which is learned behaviour, or they understand what is expected of them. This is why the most important step in developing leaders is ensuring they fully understand what good looks like. This is about ensuring there is a leadership framework they understand with clear values and leadership behaviours detailed with the right solutions available for their development.

This is the 'Leadership Architecture' required to develop leaders, that provides understanding as well as a level of accountability to self-serve and build their own development plan. This should be supported through on the job assessment and coaching. In the times we live, remote leadership is now key and although it is very different to what most have known in the past, the key principles of leadership still apply.

The mistake some organisations make is to think they have defined leadership, when actually if you ask their leaders what good looks like, not many can actually really explain or understand why they are the behaviours in the first place. What this can lead to is leaders making it up as they go along, dysfunctional leadership and countless vendors providing reactive leadership development services, which in most cases is not solving the problem other than ticking the development box, however good the solution.

Human-Centred Leadership

To build on the generational development of leadership, the need for human-centred empathetic leadership during the pandemic age as emotional intelligence, has never been more important where a leader demonstrates they care, are committed, and can be trusted.

Human leadership where empathy, compassion, humility and respect are the required behaviours, when leading people through the times we now live in. And strong leadership is still required to make the tough decisions and take the actions that matter. Albeit a lot of decisions leaders will have no power as we see more divestment, redundancies, closures, mergers, and acquisitions.

Before the pandemic, we were beginning to live in times were people expected to be empowered and given autonomy, albeit with the millennials coming through, so a leader had to be nurturing whilst giving individuals freedom. Those leaders who could create leaders in their own right, so they can be themselves and lead creatively, would be the future of leadership.

But we never saw the pandemic age coming, which is a powerful reminder that leadership is about helping others dream more and be more. A leader comforts, supports and takes the blame when things are going wrong and then takes a step back out of the light when things are going right. Visible leadership is required right now.

In the old world when recruiting leaders before the pandemic there were three key areas which were important.

The first is do they have a passion for being a leader who wants to make a difference in the organisation, in people's lives, and in essence, whether they care. The second is do they have the capability to become the leader you are looking for in your organisation. Many believe that anyone can become a leader, but you need to take into consideration the working landscape, the new normal and impacts of the future to understand if an individual will be able to be a leader in your organisation. Think how many subject matter experts have been promoted to leader but not been up to the task. And the third aspect is their outlook; how positive, adaptable, and resilient they are as a person.

When you bring together their passion, capability, and outlook you will have great potential for leadership, and this is still just as important when recruiting leaders today.

But when we look at the future, we really do need to ensure leaders are human-focused, empathetic, authentic, have a real sense of purpose, a growth mindset and are able to demonstrate learning agility. We really do need to dig deeper under the surface to ensure we are recruiting for the right leadership qualities.

What will be critical in this is a leader's mindset, how they measure up and live by the values and leadership model or framework of the organisation.

Some organisations will think they have defined their values and leadership model, but in some cases when it is cascaded down, no one buys into the model. The question is: have they completed research based on analytical data, qualitative measures, unbiased opinion, external research and leadership experts as well as involving everyone in the process? Ensuring leaders understand the thinking behind the values, behaviours or changes is essential if you want to change behaviour or create the desired leadership behaviours in the organisation.

Like anything, if you want to decorate your own house you can, but when you bring in the professionals you are guaranteeing your results and your house then looks immaculate. The same can be said of buildings - if you take time to create detailed plans and build a solid foundation, you will create and build a magnificent building, which is how some of the tallest skyscrapers and exquisite buildings have been built to date. The same principles apply to leadership; you define it to shape the leaders of the future today.

Getting ahead starts by shaping the future now, by making the changes so when we are faced with the next burning platform, it is a transitional process instead of an eruption that threatens the very core of organisational and human existence. We need leaders to lead the way and the mindset of those leaders is where we start, with human-focused leadership and leaders who understand the power of special attention. The future of leadership is mindsets rather than simply competencies. However, bringing them both together is the key.

A Quick Reminder:

- The Hawthorne Effect describes the increase in performance of individuals who are noticed, watched, and paid attention to by researchers or supervisors.

- 'Special Attention' motivates people.

- Organisations need to take a step back, to rethink ways of working and what leadership means, and to ensure they have leaders who can create the culture they desire, along with developing their people to meet the demands of now and the future.

- Your leaders will create your culture which in turn impacts behaviour and results.

- If leaders are not provided with the guidance and understanding of how to lead, how to be a leader, and what leadership means, then they can make simple mistakes and demonstrate dysfunctional behaviours.

- According to Gallup, one in two leave their job because of their manager.

- Leaders need to be developed earlier and understand what good looks like through well-thought through leadership behaviours or models and training.

- In a study by McKinsey & Co, 89% of employees were satisfied when the company delivered great leaders who are inspirational, supportive, empowering and focused on development.

- The need for human centred empathetic leadership during the pandemic age as emotional intelligence, has never been more important, where a leader demonstrates they care, are committed, and can be trusted and use special attention to motivate their people.

- The future of leadership is mindsets rather than simply competencies; bringing them both together is the key.

To Do:

- *Think about how you use special attention in everything you do and how you can use it as a motivational and productive tool as a leader or across your organisation.*

- *Review and understand your organisation's definition of leadership. If you don't know it, seek it out and if you have accountability for it or can challenge it if it needs updating, then take action.*

- *Leadership models are designed by experts, so don't just create a sticky plaster version for your organisation. Whatever you do, keep it simple.*

- *Within your organisational values or leadership models, ensure there is a focus on human centred leadership.*

- *If one in two people leave their jobs in general because of their manager, invest in leadership development to ensure they are trained as new leaders to understand and role model what good looks like for your organisation.*

- *Consider what type of mindset you expect your leaders to have and redefine what it means to be a leader for your organisation.*

- *Combine mindsets and competencies to think different and create the leader of the future today.*

The Big Idea:
Human-centred leadership – we all have responsibility to develop and create leaders the world now wants to see.

A Leadership Lesson from the Elephants

"People are so difficult. Give me an elephant any day." - Mark Shand, British travel writer and conservationist.

Elephants are graceful animals who stay together in herds, normally led by a matriarch leader in the pack. The elephant is the world's largest land mammal, with some males on average measuring up to 3m high and weighing up to 6 tonnes.

Elephants can live up to 70 years old and they have around 150,000 muscle units in their trunk. The elephant's temporal lobe (the area of the brain associated with memory) is larger and denser than that of people - hence the saying 'elephants never forget'. Elephants are intelligent and are known for their cooperation and working effectively as a team. When a problem presents itself, the herd come together to solve the problem and also to defend the herd. Each elephant may have different skills, but they come together especially as they strategically move across the savannah in search of food and water.

Elephants will take their time, step back and where possible reflect on their options before taking well-thought through action. The herd who sticks together, survive and thrive together. And although each elephant will have its own personality, they share a common bond and empathy that is human-like.

Habitat: Elephants are found most often in savannas, grasslands, and forests but occupy a wide range of habitats, including deserts, swamps, and highlands in tropical and subtropical regions of Africa and Asia.

There are now only approximately 40,000 left in the wild.

Elephants are classified as an endangered species.

5

A Leader's Mindset

Avoiding the Leadership 'Pygmalion Effect'

The mindsets that leaders will require in the future

> *"Understand the Pygmalion Effect: Leaders should always expect the very best of those around them. They know that people can change and grow."*
>
> – Warren G. Bennis, American writer and pioneer of the field of Leadership Studies

In 1968, an experiment was conducted by psychologists Robert Rosenthal and Lenore Jacobson in Oak Elementary School in San Francisco. Teachers were told that the students were being given a test measuring *"potential academic spurters."*

Once the test was complete, the top 20 performers' names were given to the teachers as the high performers. However, what the teachers didn't know, was the top 20 had been picked randomly and the test could not identify potential. The teachers focused their efforts on those top 20 and set easier competence tasks for those they thought were the lower performers.

What happened?

Eight months later, the top 20 were re-tested; they had significantly improved their scores on the test. The self-fulfilling prophecy of providing the right attention meant that their performance greatly improved.

The power of the teachers' expectations influences the student performance and the corresponding attention given, impacts performance either positively or negatively, dependent upon those expectations.

Rosenthal and Jacobson originally described the phenomenon as the 'Pygmalion Effect'. Subsequently, in their 1985 paper, Rosenthal and Elisha Babad commented,

"When we expect certain behaviours of others, we are likely to act in ways that make the expected behaviour more likely to occur."

When we think about leadership in this context generally, we tend to make our first impressions of people in the first 7 seconds. We then also tend to back up our first impression by looking for evidence to support our assumptions. The same rings true with people's performance - once we have decided they are a high, medium, or low performer, we then never usually change our minds except in exceptional circumstances. We normally find it easy to pigeonhole and stereotype people. This can be due to a lack of appreciation of diversity or shortcomings of the leader themselves.

What is amazing is thinking about the power of the teacher or leader's mindset, how they treat others and then in turn, how that impacts on results. If we actually stop for a minute and think about how our mindset then impacts our own life along the way, we think the same will ring true. The importance of how we think is beautifully summarised by this quote…

"The quality of your thoughts will determine the quality of your life." A.R. Bernard, American pastor and life coach

A Leader's Mindset

When you think about leadership now, there have never been more changing factors which influence how to be a successful leader. Whether that be through the hierarchical system of organisations, being a business leader, or leading in your own right, leadership is a myriad of challenges that requires good decision-making and resilience to succeed. Leaders are now exposed to so many internal demands and external influences, especially in regulated environments, along with people and process issues, it is difficult for them to keep up.

This can create blind spots due to the pace of work, conflicting demands, and leadership by process. Leaders can also find themselves in chaos being pulled from pillar to post, but at all times their people will look for consistency in behaviours and action. They will also look for certainty in a very uncertain world, especially during these times of pandemic and change.

Where possible, leaders need to provide that certainty, but where certainty is not possible, as a minimum, must show positive behavioural consistency and a leadership mindset. 'Be a leader' being the maxim, coming from setting the example as a role model, and a genuine desire to help and support people during these times. A growth mindset, seeing their people as diverse, and talent with a fresh opportunity to impress year on year, compared to a fixed mindset, is critical to their success.

From McKinsey & Co's research, four key leadership behaviours were identified as the ones that get leaders 90% of their results in the workplace;

- Be supportive
- Operate with strong results orientation
- Seek different perspectives and
- Solve problems effectively

This was determined through the research with 189,000 people in 81 diverse organisations, based on 20 distinct leadership traits. The collaborative collective achieves more through the support and facilitation of the leader. This survey is from 2015, so what has changed in the world of leadership in those five years and what does the future bring for leadership now that we need to take into consideration?

Well, we have experienced more change in the last few years than we had known in the previous twenty; the pandemic, new ways of working, more demands on time, less time for tasks, gig leadership, technological advancements with the onset of AI, and even more multi-tasking that makes the role of a leader more complex in the future. But that depends on how you see it, as any leader will still have the same amount of time in a day, which means leaders will need to cut through the complexity to establish winning habits in the time they have, to be successful. Navigating change is and will continue to be the norm, so personal effectiveness will be critical in striving for success, whilst utilising both new technologies and people to collaborate effectively.

What rings true with leadership if you want to be effective? You have to have a passion for actually being a leader with a desire to help others. Leaders should put their people's agenda before their own.

As Simon Sinek says, *"When we help ourselves, we find moments of happiness. When we help others, we find lasting fulfilment."*

Add to that the fact that people don't buy what you do, they buy 'why' you do it, which is found in a person's reason for actually being a leader in the first place.

The importance of allowing team members to shine when they are producing brilliant work, and then being visible when things go wrong to ensure you have their back, will always be the best way to set a good leadership example. Some things don't need to change when it comes to leadership.

Part of the leader's purpose is to remain human in a world increasingly reliant on technology and processes. But it is that genuine purpose in helping and empowering others which should be at the core of being a leader. But then how many people get management or leadership wrong would you say? Have you left a boss who micromanages or whose values are not aligned with yours?

An example of dysfunctional leadership is someone who switches their political interests to become a leader of a political party where they may now be in a better position to win the vote, but it goes against the reasons they got into politics in the first place. Their 'why' is purely in their own self-interest, not that of helping others and putting their country first. Too often we now see politicians only interested in their own agenda and some will switch allegiance from one position to an opposing position if it will get them in power. The lies and deceit of politicians is incredible but even with this lack of integrity, people still vote for their chosen party. Politics just provides the backdrop to a dysfunctional setting that is easy to draw upon when it comes to the classic example of manipulative, command-and-control style leadership or a "I don't care as long as I have, or I am in power" attitude. Mentioning no names, I am sure you get the point! This is leadership basically moving backwards in time instead of progressing forwards, but then maybe I'm missing the point here expecting leadership to be about doing something good in the world instead of a leader's personal agenda…

And I'm sure there are many more people who are leaders with positive intentions, who are just looking to navigate the murky waters of the continual flow of information and the pressures of work in a society that feels like it is becoming more dystopian by the day. The pandemic has created a new norm for work so what about creating a new style of leadership?

So how do we think like a leader in a changing world? If leaders are to sufficiently navigate and lead through change, 'purpose' is what defines a leader, along with a step change in mindset. We live in times where integrity, respect, and decency need to cut through the jungle of misinformation, so not only can we thrive in business, knowing we are collectively doing the right thing, but also knowing we are adding value for future generations. A leader's mindset is critical to this and being able to deal with the exponential change we will all continue to face. As Korn Ferry, the leadership specialists, call out in The Third Wave, leaders now need Agency, Authenticity and Agility to be successful in the times we live, as mentioned in Chapter 2.

To build upon this and navigate change here are a number of mindsets required for the leaders of today to be successful. This is based on 30 years' research and comes from my previous book, Reframe Your Mindset: Redefine your Success.

It is important to understand firstly that a growth mindset is essential to a person's success, but it is not this mindset alone that makes people successful; it is a combination of different mindsets that make people successful including a growth mindset.

Aspiration Mindset

"If a thing is humanly possible, consider it within your reach" – Marcus Aurelius, Roman Emperor and philosopher

An aspiration mindset is more than a growth mindset - it is the ability to think big, to believe you can create your future and step into it. From a leadership perspective, it is ensuring that you have a sense of purpose for being a leader, connecting to the bigger picture, both in your organisation and out into the world.

Being a leader is about how you add value to others and the organisation, which is the essence of leadership, wrapped in purpose-driven behaviours. It is about understanding why you work where you do, ensuring that it matches your values, making sure you have that purpose as a leader to make a difference and help others. It is about helping and supporting others to be their best or to be a leader in their own right within the organisation to help shape the future. The leader's aspiration in this day and age, should be to create leaders.

But it is also in a world that requires positive change a mindset that thinks big beyond oneself, one's organisation and to creating impacts in the world that are far-reaching. Through helping others in need of help, working towards a sustainable future, making the right decisions to save the plant from climate change, to as big a purpose as working towards the UN Global goals to drive positive change in the world. We can all make a difference, no matter how small, just as interest in the bank that compounds over years of saving to make a much larger sum. As environmental activist Greta Thunberg says, "No one is too small to make a difference" and the difference we can all make to the future can and will have a massive impact.

An 'Aspiration Mindset' is one of agency, sense of purpose and meaning for what you do as a leader.

Belief Mindset

"Human beings have an innate inner drive to be autonomous, self-determined, and connected to one another. And when that drive is liberated, people achieve more and live richer lives." – Daniel Pink, American best-selling motivational author.

A belief mindset is about having self-belief and conviction for who you are and what you are capable of doing. As a leader, it is about enhancing the mindset of others and building their self-belief. Empowering your people to give them freedom, autonomy and trust, demonstrates a belief mindset when leading others. Naturally it may be more difficult in some environments but treating your people like adults generally means they act like adults. Treat them like children and guess what you get? Contrary to popular belief, autonomy drives accountability, so when we treat people as adults, they behave as such. Treat them like leaders whom you trust with responsibility, accountability, and ideas, then you will maximise your results and have the freedom to focus more strategically on what you do.

The secret to motivating others is simple. It is genuine special attention and when you treat someone like a leader, where you listen and show genuine interest allowing freedom of expression, you will quickly notice how positively they respond. Yes, some people need more clarity of instruction, some may need more feedback and coaching through your support, some may need you to lead until they feel they can be outright leaders themselves, but then helping them get there is why you are a leader in the first place. Our brains are wired to self-direct, so let your people make their choices and trust them to make the right ones. Most senior executives consider themselves as great leaders, yet 79% of employees said they'd been victims of micromanagers.

Your people will feel more valued when an organisation promotes autonomy. If the culture you create is one of freedom, creativity and innovation, then your culture will be so much better for it. This 'Belief' Mindset instils your trust in your team and the best way to this is empower them and give them autonomy.

But also check in and make sure they do not feel like they have taken on too much or feel like they are in a place of Imposter Syndrome. We now know that imposter syndrome affects up to 70% of people at some time in their lives and more so those who find themselves in leadership positions. There is an opportunity when leading people to develop their self-talk and to build their self-esteem. A powerful message from Dr. Fred Johnson shared in his TEDx Talk "I am Enough", can be the start to move away from the negative thinking patterns of not being good enough. Helping your people to re-wire and reframe their thinking will be essential to their success, especially in the times we now live. I'm sure that at times through the pandemic and lockdown when learning new ways of working, we have all felt some form of imposter syndrome or lack of confidence.

We also need to understand that if our people hold self-limiting beliefs, it will hold them back so identifying those beliefs and replacing them with empowering ones will strengthen their mindset and resolve. The following well-known story illustrates how conditioning and belief can hold power over everything we do…

"As a man was passing the elephants, he suddenly stopped, confused by the fact that these huge creatures were being held by only a small rope tied to their front leg. No chains, no cages. It was obvious that the elephants could, at any time, break away from their bonds but for some reason, they did not.

He saw a trainer nearby and asked why the animals just stood there and made no attempt to get away. "Well," the trainer said, "when they are very young and much smaller, we use the same size rope to tie them and, at that age, it's enough to hold them. As they grow up, they are conditioned to believe they cannot break away. They believe the rope can still hold them, so they never try to break free."

Remember that how we think of our people and therefore act towards them can, without knowing, either make them feel like they are an imposter or brilliant at what they do. One of the greatest things a leader can do is build the self-belief of others. So firstly, work on your own self-belief and in turn, use those lessons to help the people you lead build their own.

What is also important with a belief mindset is what we can achieve as a collective group; what is possible when we bring the right people together and how we can make positive change for our people, our organisation and once again out into the world. When you have the power to be able to bring people together or lead a team of leaders, then it is always possible to achieve more. And you can make this happen by building the belief of the team.

A 'Belief Mindset' as a leader is one that empowers and trusts, giving your people autonomy to collaborate, innovate and act as leaders.

Drive Mindset

"When it's tough, will you give up or will you be relentless?" – Jeff Bezos, American entrepreneur and founder of Amazon

Those who are successful have drive and the motivation to succeed. If we think about aspiration as having the vision and big goals through planning, then drive is about the energy and motivation you have to act, and belief that you can succeed. When we translate this to leadership, it is about identifying and supporting your people to succeed and achieve their goals.

When leading people for the first time, it is always important to assess an individual's capability and their drive and motivation. If they have both, then you know for all intents and purposes, they have what they need to succeed. If they don't, then coaching to build their capability is possible, but it is far more difficult to develop their drive and motivation. This is about really finding out what their meaning and purpose are and matching it as closely as possible to develop a 'Drive' mindset which is relentless in taking action.

Jeff Bezos launched Amazon as an online bookstore from his garage in 1994. Part of his success has been about learning from failure and being able to turn that into positive momentum. His desire, drive and motivation kept him going, even when on numerous occasions he failed. Amazon now makes billions of dollars, and it is an example of what is possible with the right drive and determination to succeed. Many of us may not want to create a billion-dollar company but whatever our goals are, as a leader it is important to be driven and where possible, to motivate or push others to succeed. When developing your leaders, it will be meaning and purpose that will be the decisive factor that drives them towards their goals.

When a leader creates real drive within the team to reach their goals, the possibilities and what can be achieved are amazing.

A 'Drive Mindset' is about providing the right environment for your people to feel motivated and driven to succeed.

Authentic Mindset

"Life is ten percent what happens to you and ninety percent how you respond to it." – Lou Holtz, American football coach and analyst

Leaders in the future will be judged on their authenticity and how they show genuine interest in helping others, demonstrate integrity in their decision-making, showing all people at all levels respect, and are found to be trustworthy. This can always be difficult because there will always be different types of personality at work. If we take a tool such as the Myers Briggs Type Indicator, there are 16 different types of defined personality and then millions of variations even within a type. However, sometimes type A will not trust type B purely because they see the world differently, trust and gather different sources of information, express their emotions differently, make decisions either in a subjective or objective way or like to plan or let life happen.

Working across these multiple differences takes a high level of self-awareness and emotional intelligence (EQ) with a genuine and authentic commitment to collaborate and listen. It was Lou Holtz, former American football player, coach, and analyst who explained that to build great relationships as a leader, you need to demonstrate you care, that you are committed to your people's agenda and that you can be trusted. This in itself is a test for every relationship you have; if you can answer yes to all three, then you have a great relationship. What is it built upon? Genuine interest in helping others rather than engineering or duplicity. People can tell whether you are an authentic leader…why? Because they can feel it.

So how can organisations demonstrate authenticity? By actually living and breathing their values which is a by-product of their leader's role-modelling those values.

Over the last couple of years, we have learnt the importance of being more kind to ourselves and others, along with what it means to be human.

This is why an authentic mindset is so important because this means that you genuine do care about others, you are committed to them as people and that they will be able to trust you with their best interests. After all, isn't that what being human is all about?

An 'Authentic Mindset' is one of genuine kindness driven by human-centred leadership and values-based leadership.

Resilience Mindset

> "When we learn how to become resilient, we learn how to embrace the beautifully broad spectrum of the human experience." – Jaeda Dewalt, American writer and artist

We have never needed to be more resilient than in the times we now live. I'm sure during these last few years we have all faced setbacks and new challenges along the way, from being able to deal with lockdown, to having or recovering from Covid, to new ways of working. Many people have realised that it is now possible to live and work in different ways to previously, and we are now seeing 'the Great Resignation'. For some, this is now a great opportunity to find a work/life balance with more power in the hands of the employee. But whatever the future holds, leaders will be faced with the challenge of ongoing exponential change, along with leading across virtual, face to face and metaverse landscapes.

The dimensions of resilience are mental, emotional, physical, and spiritual. At times we don't actually know how resilient we are until we are challenged. What we can do is keep our resilience topped up, by considering each of these four dimensions and how we can stay optimised for the future.

If we can remain vigilant when it comes to our own resilience levels, and we understand the importance of keeping those areas optimised, we can then advise and help others be more resilient.

With all the change currently happening around us, understanding the importance of how challenged most people are, especially with ongoing economic pressures, it is important to build resilience both in your people and within the organisation.

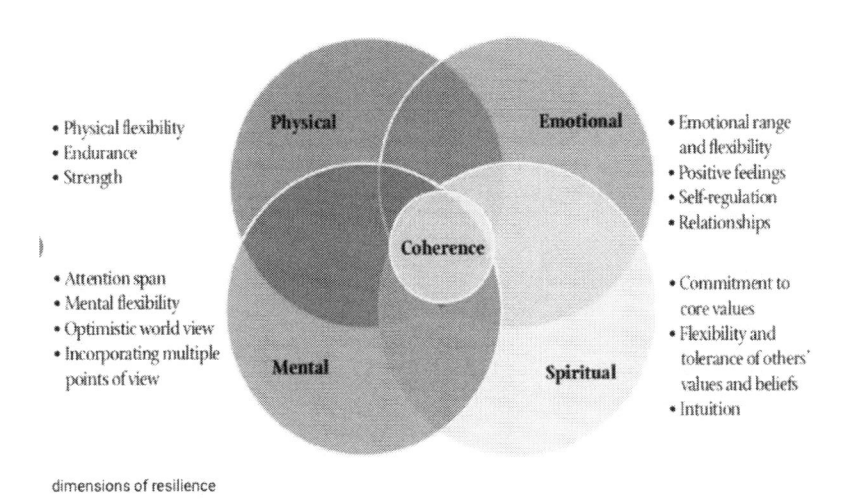

Physical
- Physical flexibility
- Endurance
- Strength

Mental
- Attention span
- Mental flexibility
- Optimistic world view
- Incorporating multiple points of view

Emotional
- Emotional range and flexibility
- Positive feelings
- Self-regulation
- Relationships

Spiritual
- Commitment to core values
- Flexibility and tolerance of others' values and beliefs
- Intuition

Coherence

dimensions of resilience

https://www.researchgate.net/figure/dimensions-of-resilience_fig2_286389941

Human-centred leadership does not mean that as a leader you go completely soft; it is still important to manage performance and use candour if unacceptable behaviours or performance persist.

This at times takes resilience itself in the face of providing what could be deemed as providing negative feedback, or the need to make tough decisions. But leaders in the future will know that to survive and thrive, they will need to optimise their mental, emotional, physical, and spiritual resilience to meet the challenges ahead.

A 'Resilience Mindset' is a leader who continually optimises their mental, emotional, physical, and spiritual resilience and helps to build those dimensions of resilience in others.

Learning Agility Mindset

"The question I ask myself like almost every day is, 'Am I doing the most important thing I could be doing?'" – Mark Zuckerberg, American media magnate, founder of Meta Platforms

Learning agility is about what your first response is to a situation, how you demonstrate the ability to successfully adapt, either based on past experience or applying novel or creative approaches to the situation. People who demonstrate learning agility have a growth mindset and are open to new ideas and ways of thinking. Because of the amount of change and complexity in work, leaders who demonstrate agility will have more success, because those that adhere to conformity will struggle to adapt. Leaders who make mistakes and try new things and who learn from failure quickly, will adapt to their changing environment better than those fixed in their ways. Hearing the words 'We have always done it this way' is a mindset prison for those moving in the opposite direction to the tide of change that is happening in the world.

The attitude of looking to continually learn and improve, along with being focused on the objective, is a clear road map for success. As Ben Hunt-Davis, the British Olympic Rower, explains in his book, *'Will It Make the Boat Go Faster?'*, the UK rowing team were not the best team, however they applied a growth mindset to one very clear objective, 'how to make the boat go faster'. If an idea made the boat go faster, they used it but if it didn't, then they didn't waste their energy. Focusing on this as a team led to Olympic Gold in Sydney 2000.

The world is changing every day so it's so much better to be shaping the future than to have your future shaped for you. Taking risks is not about taking a mindless gamble or throwing caution to the wind, it is about taking calculated risks to put yourself and others forward, try new things, be creative, suggest ideas and innovate where possible. It is about asking 'why?' and 'why not?' or 'what if?'. It is about thinking strategically about the future. It is about having vision for what is possible. It is about innovating with data to support you or using data to shape your strategy. It is also about tapping into the diversity of the group and collaborating.

As a leader, it is about facilitating other people to bring innovative ideas to the table. Let your people challenge you, challenge the convention, think differently, and shape the future together.

Thomas Edison tried two thousand different ways to make a filament for the light bulb. When none worked satisfactorily, his assistant complained, *"All our work is in vain. We have learned nothing."* Edison replied, *"Oh, we have come a long way and we have learned a lot. We know that there are two thousand elements which we cannot use to make a good light bulb."*

American inventor Charles F. Kettering, who was head of research at GM from 1920-1947, said, *"You must learn how to fail intelligently. Failing is one of the greatest arts in the world. One fails forward toward success."*

When you bring your people together to collaborate, celebrate mistakes rather than avoiding them. Failure is not a final destination, but a necessary stop along the innovation journey. When we criticise mistakes. we silence innovation. A Mistake Tolerant Mindset is a shift to 'what if?', looking at multiple scenarios and understanding that decisions have consequences and benefits but also accepting any failure along the way.

It is all part of the innovation process. It is about individual and collective learning agility and growth mindset to be able to lead and learn. When employees are not afraid of making mistakes, they're more productive and innovative at work.

A 'Learning Agility Mindset' is one of curiosity, creativity, and innovation.

When your leaders multiply these leadership mindsets with a positive outlook and overall growth mindset, they will be set up for success in the future. If you want to change behaviour, you need to change the thinking behind the behaviour. This is why mindset is so important. The right mindset plus leadership competencies based on what good looks like will propel leaders into the future to meet the megatrends and equip them for the challenges that lie ahead.

We must remind ourselves of the Pygmalion Effect mentioned above and the importance in this day and age that we need to think of our people as leaders rather than followers or subordinates.

We also need to understand they are human so to lead with human-centred leadership rather than treating people as if they are a task. We need to remember that our actions impact others' beliefs about us which in turn, causes their actions towards us and then re-enforces our beliefs about them. It is important to make sure our actions are positive ones and demonstrate respect and integrity for others. Treating your people like leaders is a sure way to ensuring you have a positive self-fulfilling prophecy to work towards developing leaders for the future.

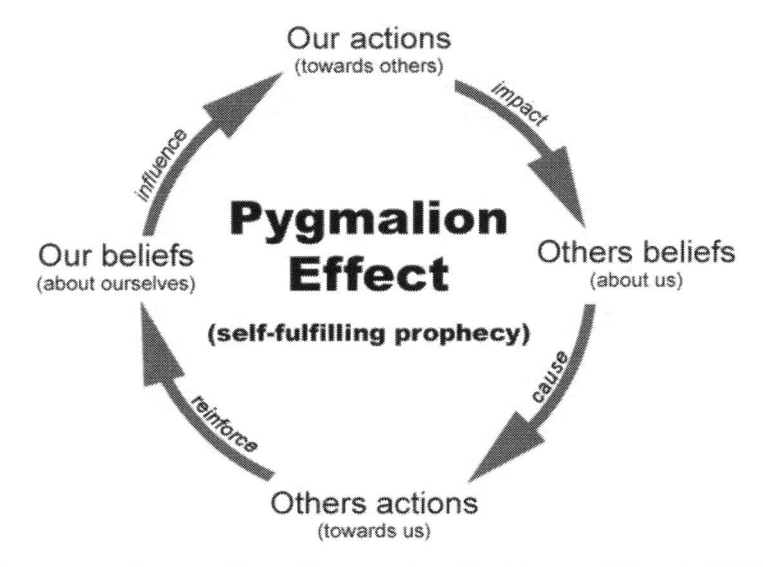

Pygmalion Effect

Our actions (towards others) → impact → Others beliefs (about us) → cause → Others actions (towards us) → reinforce → Our beliefs (about ourselves) → influence →

(self-fulfilling prophecy)

https://www.researchgate.net/figure/The-Pygmalion-Effect-Kashen-2011_fig1_331981823

A Quick Reminder

- The Pygmalion Effect - when we expect certain behaviours of others, we are likely to act in ways that make the expected behaviour more likely to occur.
- The four key leadership behaviours identified in McKinsey & Co's research, that get leaders 90% of their results in the workplace; Be Supportive, Operate with Strong

Results Orientation, Seek Different Perspectives and Solve Problems Effectively.

- It is important to understand firstly that a growth mindset is essential to a person's success. It is not this mindset alone that makes people successful, but a combination of mindsets, including a growth mindset.

- An 'Aspiration Mindset' is one of agency, sense of purpose and meaning for what you do as a leader.

- A 'Belief Mindset' as a leader is one that empowers and trusts, giving your people autonomy to act as leaders, collaborate and innovate.

- A 'Drive Mindset' is about providing the right environment for your people to feel motivated and driven to succeed.

- An 'Authentic Mindset' is one of genuine kindness driven by human-centred leadership and values-based leadership.

- A Resilience Mindset is a leader who continually optimises their own mental, emotional, physical, and spiritual resilience and helps to build those dimensions of resilience in others.

- A 'Learning Agility Mindset' is one of curiosity, creativity, and innovation.

- When your leaders multiply these leadership mindsets with a positive outlook and overall growth mindset, they will be set up for success in the future.

- If we view all our people as leaders, then we start a positive self-fulfilling prophecy through the Pygmalion Effect.

To Do:

- *Aspiration Mindset - As a leader are you in a role that aligns to your values, gives you purpose where you can make a difference or make the difference you want?*

- *Belief Mindset - How do you treat your people? Do you show genuine interest and how do you empower them to be leaders and give them autonomy?*

- *Drive Mindset – How do you create the right environment for your people to find meaning and purpose in what they do?*

- *Authentic Mindset - How do you appreciate the diversity in your team, and do you demonstrate that you care, you are committed and can be trusted?*

- *Resilience Mindset – How do you optimise and build the dimensions of resilience for yourself and your team?*

- *Learning Agility Mindset - How open are you to looking to learning to enhance and improve what you do with clear focus on your objectives?*

- *Your Outlook – Do you have a positive, adaptable and growth mindset outlook?*

- *Rate yourself or your leaders on each of these mindsets out of 10 with 10 being high and 1 being low. What are your strengths? What mindsets do you need to develop further? How do your leaders' rate?*

- *How are you treating your people like leaders?*

The Big Idea

Based on the uncertainty and exponential change in the world it is important for leaders to treat their people like leaders. Having the right leadership mindset will be critical to developing the leaders the world now wants to see and ensures a positive self-fulfilling prophecy.

A Leadership Lesson from the Tiger

"The tiger will see you a hundred times before you see him once." -
John Vaillant, American/Canadian author

The tiger is the world's biggest cat and the top predator in its food chain. They are easily recognizable with their dark vertical stripes and orange fur but in their natural habitat it helps to camouflage their attack. The tiger is the ultimate introvert as all adult tigers live alone. But this has its drawbacks as tigers are only 5% likely to be successful in their hunt compared to lions, who hunt in packs and are successful 25% of the time.

Tigers stalk their prey with complete focus, keeping their eye on the goal and knowing that the slightest sound may disturb their prey. Tigers are known to hunt once every eight to nine days and have learnt to go long periods between meals but also due to their low success rate, show persistence in the hunt. Being patient and focused like the tiger is an important leadership skill we can learn.

Tigers are very intelligent animals, and they adjust their hunting tactics dependent upon prey. Traditionally, they will kill prey by attacking the neck but when hunting crocodiles or even bears, they have learnt to change their strategy. Being a lone predator demonstrates how capable they are of adapting to their surroundings as well as demonstrating learning agility to ensure their survival.

As leaders we can learn a number of key lessons from the tiger about developing a growth mindset, learning agility, being able to adapt to our surroundings, being persistent and focused on the task at hand.

Habitat: Tigers are found in diverse habitats: rain forests, savannas, grasslands, rocky areas, and mangrove swamps in Asia.

93% of historical tiger lands have disappeared because of human expansion in the world and there are 3,900 estimated numbers still alive in the wild.

Tigers are an endangered species.

6
The Mindset of an Organisation

What if the organisation was human?

Create organisations we can relate to for the future

> "You have to look at leadership through the eyes of the followers and you have to live the message. ~ Anita Roddick, British businesswoman and environmental campaigner

In a highly controversial 1971 Stanford University study led by Dr. Philip Zimbardo, a research team replicated a prison environment in the university basement where paid volunteers, screened for being "psychologically stable," were randomly grouped into prisoners and guards. In a remarkably short period of time, the prisoners and guards slipped into stereotypical roles with the prisoners becoming submissive to the increasingly bullying and sadistic guards. The experiment quickly got out of hand and was stopped after just six days.

The Stanford Experiment explains the situational component of human behaviour and how people quickly conform to negative roles, irrespective of their personal code of ethics. The average large workplace tends to have clearly defined roles and hierarchies. Leaders who allow authority to go to their heads can rapidly create a negative culture of control and submission.

This controversial experiment reminds leaders and leaders-of-leaders, that leaders set the culture and tone of the organisation and that they need to create a constructive and harmonious environment where co-workers feel engaged and productive.

Can organisations be like a human?

Following on from the Covid-19 pandemic and experiencing lockdown, we have all started to think a little differently about life, the way we work and how we work as human beings. For some there has been an awakening and for others a dawning realisation that we should be kinder to ourselves and others. For most people, the dawning realisation that they can work from home and there is more to life than living countless hours in the office. What we are also experiencing is the rapid rate of and rise of new technology, which as we have seen when exploring the megatrends, will begin to further shape the lives we live in an even more profound way.

What we do know is that as part of this technology to make robots, bots, and AI more human, our scientists and inventors are exploring what it means to be human. Interestingly, at a time when we ourselves have gone through the exponential change, we have all been questioning what it means to be human in the world we now live.

How does this then translate into leadership? If we go back to the start, when I questioned the morality of our world leaders, now is the time to start building the leaders the world really wants to see. In fact, we now understand that a human-centred approach to leadership is what is needed at this moment and will continue to do so in the future. We will need to be more human than the robots, although in time as we become more robot-like, and robots become more human-like will we be able to tell the difference?!

During the pandemic, was your natural position to become more human and kinder or like Zimbardo's experiment, did you become more coercive, stressed, and maybe even reverting to command-and-control? A question perhaps for both employees, leaders, and the organisation itself.

This takes me to the fundamental moment of this book - **the importance of the mindset of an organisation.** So, how do you know the mindset of the organisation? Some might say from what it does, produces or sells, and they could be right. We could perhaps know from the company values and the code of conduct it expects from its employees. Maybe from the company's leadership model, in setting expectations for leaders, or perhaps the company's business strategy and purpose. If the company's purpose is defined, that is usually pretty close to explaining the mindset of the organisation. All of the above can add up to describe different facets of the company's mindset.

But let me ask you: if you were to describe your company's mindset, what would it be? And do you like it? Are you in association and agreement with it? More importantly, is it a mindset that is congruent with the one you want to work with and be associated with? If you were to ask any leader what they felt was the mindset of your organisation, what would they say? Would you all agree? Or would it be different across the organisation?

It would be interesting to see whether what the employees think matches that of the CEO and the Executive team. The beliefs your employees will have will mean there is an organisational mindset that creates the overall culture. When this is congruent you see growth, engagement, increased performance, and satisfaction, acknowledged by your employees as an organisation which is a great place to work.

When the mindset of the organisation differs at different hierarchical levels, that is when you see barriers to the strategic plan. There are naturally other internal and external factors at play.

Internally, the past and present organisational conditioning will impact along with structures, policies, procedures, systems, or processes that are not keeping up with the pace of change or that create barriers to growth. From an external perspective, the market, regulatory codes and the pace of technological change will all influence. But barriers can always be overcome if the people have the right mindset to deal with change and the obstacles in their path.

Assessing to identify the mindset of the organisation is key to success, and in some respects is aided by employee satisfaction surveys, because they reveal the barriers and enablers to growth in the mindset of your people. However, the true measurement needs to assess what mindset employees and leaders think the organisation has in comparison to their own mindset, to see if it is congruent at all levels.

According to Schein (1995), subculture is the segments of culture which show different norms, values, beliefs, and behaviour of people due to difference in geographical areas or departmental goal and job requirements (within organisations). And it is these subcultures that can lead to cottage industries and completely different mindsets within organisations, so it is important to assess, understand and then provide the right development and communication to align leaders to move in the same direction.

If you want to change behaviour, you have to change the thinking behind the behaviour.

Leadership Challenges

Based on research into organisational challenges along with the changing technological and economic landscape, we find that most are concerned about the following in different proportion dependent upon the organisation:

- Uncertainty about the future
- Relentless ongoing transformation
- Technological and digital change
- Globalisation
- Recruiting, developing, retaining talent
- Climate change
- Regulation and compliance
- The competition inside and outside own industry
- Customer service, employee, and human experience
- The call to see organisations as both the implements of societies and the institutions which shape the societies that use them.
- Organisational conditioning

No matter what level of challenge, issue, or problem an organisation is facing, the immediate stance should always be what can be controlled. Strategic plans for 'hypothetical' futures are based on multiple scenarios for what is not controllable, with 'definite' futures defined for the controllables to make the strategic vision and plan happen.

Naturally, there are so many variables in play, where one organisation's burning platform is survival, another's is to grow at pace, and in both scenarios the mindset or capability of its leaders will be critical to its success.

Horizontal and vertical development are key, but it will be the mindset of its leaders who will be able to either cope with the pressures and stress of uncertainty, and/or demonstrate the resilience to deal with relentless transformation and change.

However, if their mindset is not congruent with the mindset of the organisation, it may slow down and impact growth.

For any organisation looking to grow, move forwards or survive, then it is important to understand its organisational conditioning to identify internal barriers. Once identified, collaborative leadership can work to resolve and shape the future of the organisation. Being part of the solution and mission will make a massive difference, to drive employee engagement, and help individuals and leaders develop an understanding of the organisational landscape.

Cultural Architects and Leadership Influencers

Leadership Influencers	Cultural Architects
Selected Leaders known for their passion and influence across the business when it comes to leadership. They influence the shaping of the strategy and provide insight to content/discussion on the social media platform that supports your leadership development.	Your 'change champions' within the business at every level who have the right energy and enthusiasm to drive positive change across the business. Where Leadership Influencers are thinkers, the Cultural Architects are the doers.

In driving towards your desired culture, a recommendation is to have cultural architects and leadership influencers who are advocates at every level willing to make things happen. This is about a group of leaders who influence the thinking, and a group who make things happen in the organisation.

Part of their purpose can be to define leadership for the organisation, while role-modelling behaviours and providing inspiring content or messages through company social media and communication, whilst also acting within the business as the deliverers of change and communication and to embed this across the organisation. They form an important part of the overall leadership architecture for making things happen and develop the thinking across the organisation.

Their peers see the right level of energy from people they work with daily, which all helps to embed the desired culture and enhance employee engagement. Leadership can be made very simple, however, being a leader within organisations with the complexity of the challenges scales up the responsibility and pressures faced. Ensuring your leaders are supported, developed, and empowered means challenges can be met positively and overcome. With their innovation, the future will be shaped.

But here is the thing… when we talk about this concept of the mindset of the organisation as something that can be surmised by the make-up of the organisation, its CEOs and Executives, Values, Purpose and so on… we could be making assumptions which would be a grave mistake. We need to clarify how it's done.

The Mindset of an Organisation

If your organisation were a human being, what would its mindset be?

How would you describe it?

And why would other people working in the company associate with it?

You bring all the information discussed above that we would normally surmise this with, you bring the CEO, Execs, Leaders at all levels, Leadership Influencers, Leadership Architects, and you discuss this in detail to get to a clear understanding of what the mindset of the organisation is. And if it were human this is how it would think.

So now let's do the sell! I won't name the organisation in this instance, but I worked with an organisation who yes, wanted to make profit, but also did a lot for the local community and supported local charities with a genuine care. The CEO and leadership team demonstrated a great deal of transparency, respect and integrity and it was felt across the organisation and matched the values. So just from that small amount of information, you start to get a feel for the mindset of the organisation.

I worked for another company who made it clear they were not about supporting good causes; it was about becoming number 1 in the market and being known as the best. The CEO and leadership team did not follow their own values and there was a lot of chaos, change, people in and people out. Straight away, you get the mindset of the organisation. Is it one you relate to?

Which of these had the highest turnover of staff? Lowest employee engagement score and lowest advocacy? It's not a difficult question is it! You may ask, why is it so important to understand the mindset of the organisation? Because in both cases it can be quickly turned around. Perhaps both companies have a buy out or a new leadership team who think differently. The impacts are either negative or positive. Employees with too much change find it difficult to relate even if it is positive, if it is changing all of the time.

With your company strategy, values, purpose, business plan, cultural artefacts, and leadership model, what should be at the very start and top of that list is the **mindset** of an organisation. It should be described and made clear to everyone in the organisation. Take Apple: if we ask their employees what is the mindset of Apple what do you think they will say? It is about innovation, it is about new smart technology the customer doesn't even know they need, it is about creating positive change for the customer and doing it in a sustainable way. The mindset of innovation hits home more than anything and guess what? Most employees know what Apple's mindset is and they relate to it, and it is congruent for every employee. The rest speaks for itself. However, that is not the case for many organisations, which is why it should now be a fundamental part of what the CEO and the organisation should define for its employees.

This may seem ridiculous to some or quite radical thinking, but now is the time to start thinking differently. We should stop thinking about organisations as things and start thinking about them as live eco systems. If we can make the organisation more human, the rest will follow.

Why?

- Because we now live in a different world
- Because it provides transparency for employees
- Because it is a massive motivating factor
- Because the organisation is showing it is human in its thinking
- Because it creates congruency for employees

- Because congruency creates results and develops culture

- Because it is time to think differently about organisations

So here is the opportunity which we can take back even further…if your organisation was a human being before we even agree on their mindset what are they like as a person? How would you describe them? Are they male or female? Where do they live? What is their personality like? Are they popular? Do they have friends and family? What do they think? How do they feel about life? Are they kind? Do you like them? What makes them most human?

If a scientist or inventor were making an organisation, they would ask these questions just as they are at the moment when thinking about what it is to be human to develop AI and robots. My point is that surely in a world that is crying out for humans to be more human, we should also be asking the same of our organisations?

In a world that is changing at such a rapid pace, with both employees and consumers being provided with more choice, if your organisation is not human or becoming more human to provide meaning and purpose for people who work there, then why should they work for you? Yes, there will always be those who just need a job but in the future these jobs will most likely be automated.

For individuals to find meaning and purpose in what they do, to work for an organisation that matches their values and whose mindset is one they believe in and are inspired to work for, will be essential. If that is not the case they will experience some kind of dissatisfaction in the role they are in and ultimately this impacts the team, function, and organisation. The danger is that we quickly fall into dysfunctional behaviours and, as with the Stanford Experiment, revert to type in a difficult situation.

From the onset of the pandemic, most organisations knew they had to change and adapt in a more human way; otherwise expectations would not be met and people would leave if they were not treated correctly. This has been the initial step in developing a much stronger psychological contract with employees and realising the importance of their Employee Value Proposition. Now it is time for individuals to truly follow their hearts and for organisations to become human-centred systems.

A Quick Reminder

- The Stanford Experiment explains the situational component of human behaviour and how people quickly conform to negative roles, irrespective of their personal code of ethics.

- During the onset of the pandemic, what was your default position? Did you conform to negative behaviour and actions, or did you act in a positive, human, and kinder way?

- There are so many challenges leaders now face in this age of the pandemic - those who succeed will be the leaders with strong mindsets who will be able to either cope with the pressures and stress of uncertainty, and/or demonstrate the resilience to deal with relentless transformation and change.

- Now is the time to start building the leaders the world wants to see and with this, it is time to focus on the mindset of organisations.

- When the mindset of an organisation is congruent with how its leaders and employees see it in a positive way, that is when organisations operate at their optimum.

- To identify the mindset of an organisation we need to think of organisations as human beings.
- Now is the time to start thinking differently about the organisations we choose to work for.

To Do:

- *Ask yourself, what is the mindset of your organisation?*
- *Is it congruent with what your employees and leaders think?*
- *Is it congruent at each level of the organisation?*
- *If your organisation were human, how would you describe it?*
- *Can you make it a priority to define the mindset of your organisation?*
- *Who are your leadership influencers with the organisation?*
- *Who are your cultural architects?*

The Big Idea

Thinking of an organisation as being human and defining the mindset of an organisation, along with the importance of congruency with its employees.

A Leadership Lesson from Chimpanzees

"Watching our closest living relatives, the chimpanzees, is reading the first chapter of human-beings' adventures in this universe!"
— Mehmet Murat Ildan, Turkish novelist and thinker

Chimpanzees are highly sociable apes and share 98.7 percent of our genetic blueprint. After humans, chimpanzees are probably the most politically aware species, and they will use all the tricks of politics for power. Chimpanzee groups are ruled by a dominant male who has to continually fight for his position normally demonstrating brute strength, intelligence and forming alliances.

Successful leaders use complex leadership strategies, emotional intelligence, and alliances to maintain harmony with the group. A chimp with emotional intelligence knows how to lead the group and keep everyone on side. Being a good leader means handing out favours, from grooming to sharing food or resources. By forming alliances with other males, he can form a strong pack that will support and fight for one another. A chimp who uses emotional intelligence and leadership strategies is most likely to rise to a leadership position and then retain it.

Those leaders who have dominated through just brute force alone are normally overthrown, as coercive leadership fails to keep the group together. A leader without followers holds no power in the chimpanzee kingdom.

Chimpanzees demonstrate the importance of emotional intelligence, use of intelligence and the forming of alliances to get results to be a successful leader.

Habitat: Chimpanzees are found in savanna woodlands, grassland-forest mosaics and tropical moist forests found across central and West Africa.

Current estimates range from 150,000 to 250,000 individuals.

Chimpanzees are a lesser endangered species.

7
Culture

Dominant mindsets within the organisation

Seven Dominant Organisational Mindsets

> "If all you're trying to do is essentially the same thing as your rivals, then it's unlikely that you'll be very successful." – Michael E Porter, American academic and writer

In his book *Competitive Advantage*, published in 1985, Michael E Porter explains that organisations who have an advantage normally excel in one of three key strategies:

Customer Service, Operational Effectiveness. or Product Leadership.

This then creates a certain type of mindset across the organisation and the most successful organisations such as Apple (Product Leadership), First Direct (Customer Service), and Amazon (Operational Effectiveness) are then known for this. Porter believes that those who truly excel are renowned for their strategic intent, but since the mid-eighties, times have changed, expectations have changed, and technology is constantly changing. Therefore, it is important to consider the impacts of strategy, culture, and mindset to be a successful and sustainable organisation.

An organisation will have a dominant mindset or mindsets that will drive the culture and success of the company through their strategic intent, business strategy, and the mindset of their people.

These collective mindsets will have both positive and negative impacts on the success of the organisation, and we can determine the common pitfalls of the organisation to consider the impacts of this aligned to business strategy. This is if we actually know what the mindset of an organisation actually is, and it has been defined or recognised, rather than cerebrally embedded subconsciously in its employees. In this age where mindset is critical to the success of organisations, I have developed Porter's model further with the same view in mind. However, because we are talking now about mindsets as part of an organisation's strategic intent, you will see how they can also be combined to define successful companies and their culture.

From an organisational perspective, the mindset of your employees and leaders is critical to creating the culture you desire to ensure your organisation is successful and sustainable and in turn, maximises profitability.

The definition of Mindset is: 'A set of beliefs or way of thinking that determines one's behaviour, outlook and mental attitude.'

The definition of Organisational Mindset is: 'The way the organisation operates through its strategy, focus and communication, that gives your leaders the view of its behaviour, outlook and mindset in how it does business.'

In my previous book, *Reframe Your Mindset: Redefine Your Success,* I used an equation to define success and its key indicators. These were:

Outlook, Aspiration, Belief, Drive, EQ, Resilience and Learning Agility.

which we explored in Chapter 5. From research and observation it is a combination of these mindsets that makes someone successful. What I have also found is these mindsets translate into organisational mindsets, that we can then use to define culture and the mindset of an organisation.

This is broken down into the following organisational mindset categories:

Outlook is a dominant Learning Mindset

Learning Mindset is an organisation whose mindset is focused on the growth of their people to learn, develop, and shape the organisation.

In a recent survey, only 8% of executives felt they could see any clear results from their learning efforts. This is a startling statistic when we think about how much money goes into leadership development across organisations globally! Pixar offers Pixar University to provide learning opportunities for its people. Pixar President Ed Catmull says, "Pixar University helps reinforce the mind-set that we're all learning and it's fun to learn together." An example of how learning works is film directors develop by asking for help from a "creative brain trust" of filmmakers, which is a peer-based process. Pixar has a collaborative learning culture built on trust and knowledge- sharing, and understands that creativity of its employees is critical to its success.

Aspiration is a dominant Strategic Mindset

Strategic Mindset is an organisation who is future-thinking and strategically aspiring to be the best they can be.

In 1973, the 'Big Three' automobile companies in the USA had over 82% of the market. But due to Toyota's strategic and aggressive plan, they now have less than 50%. How did Toyota do this? They spent years researching American makers which were far more advanced and efficient than Japanese car making at the time. They developed a strategic plan that would see Toyota provide the US Market with cars at prices much lower than the American car makers could match. Toyota moved its production to the US and also focused on continuous improvement as part of their overall strategic planning. Toyota had not only aspired to capture a big proportion of US market share, but also became renowned for its reliability, demonstrating future thinking and aspiring to be the best it could be. Toyota now holds the greatest global market share of sales, with 8.5% across the world. Toyota is a first-class example of the strategic mindset of the organisation.

Belief is a dominant Tribal Mindset

Tribal Mindset is an organisation that creates belief in the cause of the organisation where their people come together as a collective force.

Generally, a tribe has a commonality which binds the group together. The commonality could be a set of values, attitudes, beliefs, or purpose. When we think of organisations that are tribal, it is easy to think of sporting organisations that have a tribal connection, from board room to manager or coach, to players and the fans.

There have been lots of examples of this through the years, a classic example being Liverpool Football Club. From the boardroom to the manager, Jurgen Klopp, to the players and then the Liverpool fans known as 'Kopites', there is truly a tribal connection at the club.

When big Champions League nights are played at the shrine of their home ground, Anfield, the crowd are renowned for being not only the loudest, creating a tribal atmosphere of passion for their team, but also for having an ability to create what is described as a '12th man'. Their connection, especially with the manager, is seen when Jurgen takes the pitch at the end of a game and fist pumps the crowd into a frenzy!

Bear in mind, that Liverpool Football Club was a club that faced bankruptcy only about 10 years ago. It was taken over by new owners FSG and gained a Premier League title, Champions League, European Cup and World Club Cup all under Jurgen and his brilliant team.

Drive is a dominant Operational Mindset

Operational Mindset is an organisation whose people are motivated operating through planning, production, and pace to get things done.

Amazon could well be the example for Customer Service, Innovation and Strategic Mindset but one thing they also do exceptionally well is operational effectiveness.

In in their own words, *"Prioritising operational performance is equivalent to prioritising the customer experience and is critical to ensuring that we maintain trust in our company.*

We maintain a relentless focus on having effective and efficient operations to improve the quality of our digital infrastructure, our products and services."

Ultimately, Amazon wants to serve their company stakeholders, including customers, employees, partners, suppliers and vendors as well as their communities.

Emotional Intelligence is a dominant Customer Service Mindset

Customer Service Mindset is an organisation focused on providing exceptional customer service and the importance of the human touch.

Disney is renowned the world over for making dreams come true, and at the heart of this, is ensuring the customer comes first. Everything at Disney in making those dreams come true is customer-focused, from the films through to Disneyworld. We discussed Walt Disney himself as a leading example of having a vision and taking that strategic vision, but Disney as a company has a customer-focused mindset first with the level of service at Disney being planned, purposeful, and consistent.

Bruce Jones, Senior Director of the Disney Institute, says, *"When our Cast Members know their primary goal is to create happiness, they are empowered to create what we like to call 'magical moments'. From our park greeters to our attraction attendants, every employee makes decisions regarding a guest interaction centred on this key theme of 'creating happiness.'"*

Resilience is a dominant Sustainability Mindset

Sustainability Mindset is an organisation that focuses on being sustainable as an organisation.

Scottish brewery BrewDog now incorporates sustainability as an essential component of its business strategy. Established in 2007, the independent brewing company has a reputation for its innovative thinking and different approach to beers. It has a sustainability plan 'BrewDog Tomorrow', a six-point plan with eco-friendly measures and ways to save the planet in its own unique way.

James Watt, Co-Founder says, *"We've made it here by shaking up brewing and crafting with a community-owned business that is 100% powered by people. This marks a new dawn, we want to make sure that we're working to inspire a new kind of business, with sustainability at its core. Real change takes time. BrewDog Tomorrow is our commitment to continuously raising the bar and setting a new standard for beer and business."*

Learning Agility is a dominant Innovation Mindset

Learning Agility is an organisation that values diversity of thought, creativity, curiosity, and innovation to allow their people to shape the future with their ideas.

Apple is the #1 innovative company in the world. The company created game-changing innovations such as the iPod, iTunes, the iPhone and the iPad and is well- known for its innovations in hardware, software, and services. CEO Tim Cook says, *"Innovation is deeply embedded in Apple's culture. We approach problems with boldness and ambition, and we believe there are no limits. Innovation is in the DNA of the company."*

What makes Apple such an innovative company is their ability to create products that the customer didn't know they needed before they needed them. Along with their deep expertise, collaboration and attention to detail make Apple a clear example of a company that focuses on Innovation. Ask Apple if Innovation is their number 1 dominant mindset and they may say different, but it is definitely in their top 3 mindsets.

Now, there are so many more organisations we could name such as Netflix, Google and Tesla so let's explore a few more examples to make the point about how organisations use a combination of these mindsets to be effective. I'm going to start with their dominant, secondary, and possibly tertiary mindset for what makes up the company's strategic intent and mindset.

Below is a list of organisations and I have made the assumptions based on what I know about each of the organisations and what comes to mind.

Organisation	Dominant Mindset	Secondary Mindset	Tertiary Mindset
Adobe	Learning	Innovation	Customer Service
Amazon	Operational	Customer Service	Innovation
Apple	Innovation	Customer Service	Sustainability
Brewdog	Sustainable	Customer Service	Innovation
Cisco	Sustainable	Innovation	
Costco	Tribal	Customer Service	
Disney	Customer Service	Innovation	
EasyJet	Strategic	Operational	
Facebook	Tribal	Strategic	Innovation
Google	Learning	Innovation	Operational
LFC	Tribal	Strategic	Customer

McDonalds	Tribal	Operational	Customer Service
Microsoft	Sustainable	Operational	Strategic
Netflix	Strategic	Innovation	Operational
Nike	Customer Service	Innovation	Strategic
Pixar	Learning	Innovation	
Tesla	Innovation	Sustainable	Strategic
Toyota	Strategic	Customer Service	Innovation

I mentioned Apple above as an example of how they may see things differently, because from their perspective it is about the customer first, then sustainability then innovation, but it will be the combination of those three that makes up the mindset of Apple as an organisation. But generally, when we all think of Apple, Innovation is what comes to mind. The only way we can know this for a fact is to actually ask the organisation themselves what order they see their dominant mindset, secondary and so on to know for sure.

But the point I am making is they will know, and from this we start to really get a feel for the mindset of the organisation and can then identify if the organisation's leaders and employees see it the same way. Is that what they experience, understand, and are bought into working for the organisation? Is it the same at every level of the organisation?

The Importance of Organisational Mindset

Understanding your organisational mindset from the view of your leaders is critical to ensuring consistency and congruence of your business strategy and how it is delivered by your people. It is important to break down the way different levels of leaders perceive your organisational mindset, so you gain an insight into how the overall collective drives how the business operates.

To understand this better is to realise that how your individual employees think will drive their behaviour, and how your collective employees and leaders think will drive your organisational behaviour, and both will create the culture based on their beliefs and ways of thinking. This collectively creates a view of the organisational mindset in play at large but also breaks it down into areas of the business. This gives insight to not only the culture you are creating but also, more importantly, identifies the opportunities to consider creating the culture you actually desire. This will in some respects become a self-fulfilling prophecy similar to the Pygmalion Effect we talked about earlier - if the organisational mindset and strategic intent is what employees buy into, then we see a positive self-fulfilling prophecy.

We explored the need for organisations to be more human but that is not the whole mindset in itself; remember it is a combination of these mindsets that make people and organisations successful. As an individual, if you want to be the best, you have to work and develop to excel in all of the mindsets. Even though this would be amazing if organisations could do this, it is understandable due to the size and scope of organisations that they focus on one or two areas they are known for instead. Organisations do need to develop every area to be successful overall but need to carefully select the mindset and strategic intent as part of their mindset for their organisation.

A Quick Reminder

- Michael E Porter explains that organisations who have an advantage normally excel in one of three key strategies: Customer Service, Operational Effectiveness or Product Leadership.

- Organisational Mindset = 'The way the organisation operates through its strategy, focus and communication that gives your leaders the view of its behaviour, outlook and mindset in how it does business.'

- There are different types of organisational mindset based on leader's mindset in the previous chapter, Outlook is a dominant Learning Mindset, Aspiration is a dominant Strategic Mindset, Belief is a dominant Tribal Mindset, Drive is a dominant Operational Mindset, Emotional Intelligence is a dominant Customer Service Mindset, Resilience is a dominant Sustainability Mindset, Learning Agility is a dominant Innovation Mindset.

- Some organisations will have a clear dominant mindset or will be known clearly for one of them.

- Each organisation will have a Dominant, Secondary, and possibly a Tertiary Mindset and strategic intent that defines the mindset of the organisation.

- For each organisation to be successful, it needs to work at all of the mindset areas, however, be known for its dominant mindsets.

- Those organisations that have mindset and leader/employee congruency will be the most successful organisations.

To Do:
- *Identify your organisation's dominant mindset*
- *What are the Secondary and Tertiary mindsets?*
- *How does this impact the overall organisational mindset?*
- *Would your leaders/employees identify the mindset of the organisation?*
- *Would there be congruence in what they think it is and what it is?*
- *How can you embed awareness to drive congruence at all levels?*
- *Does congruence differ at different levels or parts of the business?*

The Big Idea

The future belongs to those organisations who clearly articulate their mindset and strategic intent to their people and where congruence occurs with belief in the cause.

A Leadership Lesson from Dolphins

*"The happiness of the dolphin is to exist.
For man, it is to know that and to wonder at it."
- Jacques Cousteau, French marine conservationist, scientist and film-maker.*

Dolphins are cetaceans and have curved mouths, which means they always look like they are smiling. Dolphins work together for the benefit of the group, working in small teams to confuse fish and then pick them off to feed. They instinctively know working together as a team is much better than trying to achieve tasks on their own. This makes them brilliant team players and they are also great communicators.

Dolphins are highly intelligent social creatures, they are very empathetic, and they support one another especially when another in the group is hurt. Scientists have discovered that Dolphins have learned to use different techniques along with empathy and they also teach their young these techniques and tools at a young age to help them become team players.

Dolphins love to have fun and understand the importance of playing, as they have a carefree attitude and what seems to be a great sense of humour. They love playing with objects and riding the waves or creating fun amongst the group.

When we look at the Leadership within the pod, we find it is without rank or seniority and the Dolphins adapt their leadership or who the leader is, based on the situation and environment. Dolphins are the epitome of hive leadership and can shift from leader to another effortlessly – this is a brilliant example of 'egoless' leadership.

Habitat: There are 36 dolphin species found in every ocean. Most dolphins are marine and live in the ocean or waters along coastlines. There are approx. 600,000 dolphins in the oceans.

Dolphins are a lesser endangered species; however 14 types of dolphins are now believed to be endangered.

8
The Future of Leadership

How will leadership need to evolve in the future?

The next generation of leaders - Leadership 5.0
"Leadership is the art of giving people a platform for spreading ideas that work." - Seth Godin, American entrepreneur, author and speaker

Future Shock

We are very swiftly approaching an age of 'future shock' where we are seeing significant change in a short period of time which impacts individuals and entire societies. This 'future shock' is an individual's psychological state due to the accelerated rate of technological, economic, and social change which provides information overload, leaving people 'future shocked'. They feel disconnected, stressed, and disorientated by the amount of change. *Future Shock* was published in 1970 by the futurist Alvin Toffler who argued that society was going through a revolution and structural change from an industrial society to a "super industrial society". Fast forward to today and what we see is that we are in the grip of being 'future shocked' by the exponential change which appears to be happening every day as well as by the pandemic changes and technological shift about to monopolise our lives. Although as humans, we have a strong tenacity to adapt to change and move with the times, there is always an amount of time required to be able to adapt to change.

The fear that may concern us now is that whole parts of society will find themselves replaced, disorientated and 'future shocked' as artificial intelligence, robots and bots become the new "super industrial society" albeit a "super machine powered society". For the first time in our history, we have very little idea of what the world will look like in the next 50 years. The future is changing every day, but what we do know is both technology and bioengineering have a massive role to play in the way our life and society will change. The Megatrends are upon us. Will this be for the good of humankind and future leadership? We will find out as we go, as we sit on the precipice of a revolution that will change humanity forever.

When we think of the most important resources of our times, land, machines, companies, and natural resources come to mind, but politics is now becoming a struggle between cyber warfare and who controls data. The future will belong to those who monopolise our data and use this data as a resource to shape the society of the future. Eventually, we will live in a world when we need to make less decisions because these decisions are being made for us because of the way our data is being used. The frightening things is that data will know me and you better than we know ourselves! So how do we survive when we know 'future shock' has potentially already begun?

As companies become agile, so do we as individuals. We need to understand that what guaranteed us success in the past will not necessarily guarantee us success in the future. Survival of the fittest is about those who adapt the best to change and also those who are proactive, to get ahead of the curve.

As the late, great Stephen R Covey's writes in his seminal book, *Seven Habits of Highly Effective People*, in the last habit, we need to continually sharpen the saw and with a growth mindset always be looking to improve, to be open to new challenges, to try new things, to learn from failure and keep learning, so we can adapt. But more importantly, we need to look to the future to consider what that future may bring and consider the changes we can make now. Unfortunately for those who do not, they will be part of a society that is 'future shocked'- the Zoom revolution is only the onset of what is about to begin.

When looking to the future, we may consider what will happen to leadership when there is no hierarchical leadership or management in organisations. When we live in a world where AI either owns or runs the organisation we are working for and therefore has a completely flat structure of workers doing the work. Think about this as the Hive version of society similar to how bees do all of the work for the Queen who is able to sit at home and observe in readiness for the next generation to arrive, albeit in the future, for AI, the next version or upgrade to the system. When the AI that runs the organisation is more than able to lead and manage every human, cyborg and robot worker who still has a role to play, with a quantum ease through its superior intelligence. Whether a human will have power over this AI in the future or we give AI this power awaits our discovery.

If we work backwards, we need to consider two important points. As AI is developed and created to possess a greater level of intelligence, what will it mean to be human? Perhaps we need to consider that now is the time for the rise of humans? And perhaps it is also time to consider what 'Artificial Intelligence' will mean in the future. Why?

Because if AI becomes more intelligent than us humans (although we may be upgraded at the same time), I can't but think that AI will make the appropriate decisions either for the organisation or because it is the right thing to do based on super intelligent algorithms. Whether this will be the right thing to do from a human perspective in the future we will have to wait and find out. Will Homo Deus be a match for AI Deus? Who knows?

But this is the point: when I think of AI, I know instantly that it would flatten organisational structures as the right thing to do, **because it can.** We would answer to the AI who would lead and manage us all. And I'd be surprised if someone is not working on the AI programme right now that takes line management completely out of organisations, and we all report to AIM (Artificial Intelligence Management Support), known as AMY in its human form. The same AI may actually run multiple companies and be able to tap into the collective data to provide valuable insights for companies to help develop their people.

I'm sure there are Fintechs currently looking to create this software where hierarchical leadership and management is no longer required because it can become a machine-powered activity. Where then does that leave all the managers and leaders? In 'Hive' organisations, where line management is stripped out of all roles, everyone is a leader. As mentioned in chapter 4, it will be creativity, imagination, intuition, and ethics that ensure our success in the future, but 'Hive-style' collaboration will be key.

The future will indefinably require new leadership.

The Future of Leadership

We face ever increasing levels of exponential change from now into the future. We need to keep pace with changes in technology and expectations of living in an advanced digital world where it will take less to do more. What global trends will change the leadership needed at work?

Jobs will change as technology starts to take over key roles that can easily be done by robots, bots, and digital infrastructure. With this also comes a younger, much more tech-savvy generation, who will be intuitive to the technology around them. There will be new types of jobs that will require new types of skills. Undoubtedly existing skills will become increasingly redundant, and leaders will have to navigate the expectations of their people based on this new landscape of demand and supply of inter-changeable skills. We have also seen the 'Great Resignation' where people are now thinking more about who they want to work with and how they want to work.

Driverless cars will give us more time to work, to and from the office, although most will choose to work remotely or hybrid. When in the office, workers will work in shared campuses that promote wellness, cater to retail needs, and have integrated smart technology where hot-desking is the norm. With the cost of office space, organisations will see the benefit in open, shared office spaces. As we know, since the onset of the pandemic, new ways of working remotely and hybrid will become more matter of fact and services will be tailored to home working, which has become the new norm. The onset of AI and virtual reality with the incoming multiverse will create new ways of connecting, working, and socialising, with perhaps an initial resistance to the concept but a general acceptance that will integrate into the way we live our lives.

As the population increases, we will see shifts in people demographics, which will put pressure on energy resources to support the growing population. This will increase tensions between the power houses of nuclear arms, where we can only hope a conglomerate of big players police the world to keep the peace. Currently there are tensions across the globe with Russia, China and NATO bumping heads over land, strategy, territorial rights, and space and now the war in Ukraine. How long before this spills over into the war that ends all wars? We can only hope diplomacy between these powers is achievable before we create our own Armageddon.

We will live longer as scientists break the genetic code for ageing, putting even more pressure on a world of limited resources, and our human parts will be replaceable by advances in medicine. We will benefit from Artificial Intelligence but also be concerned about a doomsday scenario, where robots threaten mankind because of their advanced intelligence.

As always in a future world of ever-changing demands, new leadership will be required to ensure we continue to survive.

Change Facilitators

Leaders will connect people and ideas instead of telling people what to do and how they should be working. Future generations of employees will expect to be treated like leaders. They will want trust, autonomy, and independence.

Command-and-control leadership will be seen less and will eventually be phased out by natural selection as new generations have a style of leadership that is a product of how they see the world. This style will be empowering in a fast-paced working environment. This will not happen overnight, but the new generation of leaders will be better educated at an early age to understand that to get the most from people, you need to treat them like leaders who can be trusted. Positive psychology will become more embedded in our everyday lives. If you continue with a directive and controlling style of leadership, just like the dinosaurs were eventually replaced by the evolution of more adaptable life forms, so will the leaders who cling to old styles of leadership be replaced by future generations who see leadership for what it is.

As we have seen with the increase of home working due to the pandemic, the future will see hybrid working and the dynamic itself will create an autonomous workforce which requires leaders who excel in remote leadership. The workforce demands will create new jobs where interchangeable skills will be required, and workers will need to demonstrate a high level of learning agility. Leaders will not be able to exert power through position or expertise as the need to know everything diminishes.

This means having the ability to bring out the best in their people, working 'with' them as opposed to having people work 'for' them, will be essential to their success as a leader.

Leaders will understand the megatrends that are shaping the world and will not only be able to adapt to change themselves but will also be able to facilitate inspiration in others to adapt to the volatility, uncertainty, change and ambiguity in the world. The ability to be a change facilitator in an ever-changing world will be critical to a leader's success.

A move away from static competency models

The push towards leadership autonomy across the workplace will see a move away from static competency models to new models of leadership based on leadership success factors, outcomes, roles, strengths, and values. These new factors will focus on what good looks like, to bring the best talent into the organisation, and also develop existing leaders. The move away from the 'checking of competence' to one of 'trust and empowerment' will be a shift across all organisations, along with a move away from 'performance measurement' as we are now seeing, to focusing on the 'whole person' and how they add value to the organisation.

This will be reflected in no longer needing out of date competencies, with a new focus on what success looks like across the organisation, along with an understanding of what the talent of the future is that is required today. Leadership success factors will spread across organisations where individuals will understand what success means and associate with what good looks like, with the freedom to express themselves through these success factors. Therefore, leaders will need to be leadership success-factor role models.

These will be defined by each company with key commonalities such as Emotional Intelligence, Learning Agility, Strategic Thinking and Resilience as examples of key success factors for leaders.

A shift away from multiple, complex competencies will see a shift to a small number of leadership behaviours that leaders across the organisation can relate to. It makes leadership simple and less complex, so leaders have a shared understanding of leadership across the organisation.

Other organisations will use outcome-based models that literally focus on leadership outcomes of behaviour, or they will take key behaviours and create role-based models that leaders fully understand, so if the behaviour is to be more innovative, the role is the Innovator. These new forms of leadership model will be more creative, and fluid, enabling leaders across the organisation to fully understand expectations.

Now is the time to review an organisation's leadership model as we move into new ways of working following the pandemic. It is an opportunity to create clear models that provide simplicity and understanding to shape the leaders of the future today.

Does your leadership model need to be updated?

Purposeful Leadership

As we move into the future, 'Purposeful' leadership will be required where leaders have deeper purpose and meaning for being a leader. To be a future fluent organisation will require the mindset of the organisation to clearly be doing good and have leaders who demonstrate how the business impacts the environment, society, community, customers, employees, and stakeholders.

When organisations have that authentic purpose, employees are more likely to be engaged and driven to succeed in supporting the overall vision. The same is true for leaders in the future and the Centre for Creative Leadership (CCL) have defined six must-have traits for Purpose-Led Leadership. In their Beyond Doing Good white paper from 2022, they interviewed many C-suite leaders and board directors across Asia to uncover "... *6 mindset shifts organisations must make, as they prepare themselves for a future where purpose will play a key role in their business success, social acceptability, and talent attractiveness.*"

The six mindset shifts are:

1. *Altruism to Impact.*

Purpose-led companies successfully balance social value and economic value generation. This shift requires the purposeful leadership skill of multi-dimensional sensemaking: To think and act on multiple planes — to quickly scan potential opportunities, risks, and stakeholder expectations and deal with new world situations.

2. *Nation-Centric to World-Centric.*

Organisations must solve for global issues, but not in a rigid way, tweaking global initiatives to suit local challenges and cultures. This shift requires the purposeful leadership skill of influence: The power and the ability to personally affect key stakeholder actions, decisions, and opinions in a matrixed, multi-geography environment.

3. *Short-Term to Long-Term.*

The purposeful leadership team must navigate the paradox of short-term impact and long-term benefits, with purpose being the guiding light. This shift requires the purposeful leadership skill of courage: The ability to take appropriate action steps, even in the face of adversity and pressures.

4. *Exclusive to Inclusive.*

Inclusive growth requires an ecosystem approach, focusing on the well-being of employees, customers, suppliers, communities, and the environment. This shift requires the purposeful leadership skill of humility: Recognition and acceptance of reality through self-awareness and open-mindedness. Humble leaders have a realistic sense of their own capabilities in relation to others and the situation at hand.

5. Organisational to Personal.

For strong alignment, leaders must believe in the power of purpose, cultivate individual purpose, and ensure authenticity. This shift requires the purposeful leadership skill of inspiring others: Enhancing the potential of people in a way that works for them and encourages them to push themselves, achieve more, reach their potential, or embrace a cause.

6. Why to How.

Organisations must seek answers to "how," which involves action framework, practices, communication strategy, and alignment of purpose and culture. This shift requires the purposeful leadership skill of strategic thinking: The ability to understand an organisation's long-term strategy and come up with effective plans in line with the organisation's business objectives within the local/regional/global socio-economic-environmental context."

https://www.ccl.org/articles/white-papers/beyond-doing-good-6-mindset-shifts-for-purposeful-leadership/

Contextual Leadership

With roots dating back to Fiedler's 1978 Contingency Theory, (which states that leadership isn't uniform but for leadership style to fit the situation), contextual leadership has been one of the most trending topics in leadership research over the last decade.

Based on the current change in the world from a human perspective, a lot of people have experienced burn-out and pandemic fatigue. This has created a massive focus on health and well-being across organisations. When we understand the context behind the situation, it enables us to respond as leaders in the best possible way.

Contextual leadership is about leading and decision-making through understanding the details and context behind situations. Contextual leadership requires critical thinking, creativity, empathy, and resilience to provide context-sensitive response to all the uncertainty and change. Understanding the context of the organisation, its leaders, and people in relation to internal and external factors will be essential for leaders in the future, who will continue to face even greater rates of change and uncertainty.

Contextual leaders will focus on the detail behind relationships to understand human experiences and feelings and be able to motivate and inspire through special attention. If being purposeful as a leader will be essential in the future, so will contextual leadership as a means of successfully navigating all the changes to come.

Neuroleadership

Increasing importance will be placed on neuroleadership and understanding humans. Leaders will be educated to understand the human brain, along with the importance of the mind/body connection through neuroleadership. Insights from scientific research into the brain and positive psychology will provide a new framework for leadership and organisational development.

Advances in science will provide answers to the workings of the brain, so leaders will be informed 'why' people act the way they do. As positive psychology takes a greater foothold in the workplace, leaders will cultivate the mindset of their people with the understanding that if you get the mindset right, the behaviours will follow. This will be about a mindset of purpose and agency, where their people as leaders will know why they are here and what their unique purpose is in working for the organisation.

There will be less of a hierarchical approach, with the need to be part of the collaborated and connected workplace hive, rather than part of a hierarchical top-down structure of coercive power. And through the hive, opportunity will be available for leaders who stand out who normally might not have been noticed, which will positively impact their progression and so therefore providing greater opportunities to all.

Neuroleaders will understand the importance of neurodiversity. As we come to understand the brain more, we will be able to gain greater insights as the human body and mind becomes more wired to technology to provide insights and data.

As we look to create greater leaps into science and technology as a race, we will need to be more attuned to what it means to be human; being a neuroleader will ensure there is a significant movement to human-centred leadership.

"Neuroscience findings are helping to connect the dots between human interaction and effective leadership practices. As the mapping of the human brain continues, we can expect to learn more about how the brain functions and how leaders can use this knowledge to best lead people and organizations."
– Kimberly Schaufenbuel, American expert in neuroleadership

During the last two decades, we have gained a far more accurate view of human behaviour, and what it means to be human with the integration of psychology and neuroscience. Imaging technologies, positron emission tomography, and brain wave analysis technologies have revealed unseen neural connections in the human brain, allowing for a much greater understanding of the workings of the mind.

In the years to come we are going to learn so much more about how the brain works that we will see a move to neuroleadership practice. As we take on board more of an understanding of how to lead and get the best from people through neuroscience, integrating these lessons into how we develop leaders will be essential to keeping pace in business.

A direct link to the key skills you need

In the future it is possible that key skills will be able to be downloaded directly to the brain. Individuals will therefore already be competent, so it will be about positively stretching their skills and developing their thinking.

Leaders will therefore focus on strengths-based development. They will provide special attention to their people which will ensure their people are motivated, engaged and enthused about the work and job they do. This will mean the need to go the extra mile because if leaders don't, their talent will find it easy to leave and work anywhere across the world as the landscape becomes increasingly virtual.

Focusing on how to develop the potential of their people, conversations will move to being about how the employee can be their absolute best and help them to develop ideas in the workplace, as opposed to getting them to work hard to hit performance targets. Leaders will understand the importance of the whole person paradigm and nurture their people's potential, as opposed to giving instructions and ensuring their team members have to wait to be told what to do.

Leaders will inspire not through teaching but with their knowledge of how to provide the right experiences, resources, and challenges for their people. Once again, it will be about ensuring their team members as leaders are empowered and enabled to lead the way, focusing on positive and strengths-based development. The challenge will come when AI is seen as being able to lead better than humans themselves. This will possibly mean no leadership in the future, or no human led leadership in the future in the more sophisticated organisations and establishments.

Are we that far from a programme that will take all performance management leadership away from leaders, so they can focus on the importance of how they can use their critical talents for the organisation? How plausible is it that you will have daily, weekly, monthly, quarterly performance conversations with the company's AI-driven performance guru, that provides the coaching, support and, in time, resources to develop you?

Watch this space as the next generation of technology changes the leadership landscape forever!

The age of the 'all-knowing leader' will end

Leaders will ask questions and not need to know everything.

We have all been educated to search for the right answer to questions or problems. This has impacted our creativity as we lose our imaginative nature, because there has to be one correct answer. Logic teaches us this. Organisations are also set up to do the right thing and to look for answers: in some cases, this can create a blame culture when something goes wrong. Conformity also means that it can be painful to stand out and be different.

But with technological advances, answers are becoming a commodity as we can search the internet and use Google to find answers to almost anything with ease.

In the future, successful leaders will be those who know how to ask the right questions and also know where or who to get their answers from. They will not know everything, and their credibility will not solely be about their expertise but also about their ability to think differently, ask meaningful questions, and bring the right people or knowledge together at the right time.

As change facilitators it will be more about the power of collaboration in how they bring the right people together at the right time. Their ability to facilitate groups either face to face, hybrid or virtually will be essential to tapping into diversity of thought and ideas, to be able to move into new directions and to get things done.

The ability to ask questions that go beyond Google to challenge the AI they will be working with, will also be an essential requirement of leaders in the future.

"A leader is best when people barely know he exists, when his work is done, his aim is fulfilled, they will say: we did it ourselves."
- Laozi

Human v digital: balance of the future?

Leaders must stay human in a digital world. Being authentic will be a key recruitment driver with new ways to assess people's integrity, personality traits and intentions. Who a person is, will be equally as important as what a person can do, with brain imaging tests and stress testing for the critical jobs in the organisation.

As a world of robots and digital infrastructure take over the workplace, it will never be more important to be genuinely human in dealing with customers, along with everyday colleagues. This will be due to the ambiguous nature of customer service interactions, which require a human, rather than a robot.

How to be human will become a science in itself, as robots are programmed to become more and more human-like. As AI starts to integrate with every part of our life, it will become more difficult to differentiate between who is human and who is robot.

This will mean a greater study into neuroscience and what it means to be human. Whereas emotional intelligence was the ground-breaking leadership factor in the past, we will see a move to a new level of human intelligence (HQ). This will be a determining factor in how we recruit for leaders and the whole concept of a leader will be about those who can lead themselves or others through collaboration rather than a traditional leadership position.

Hive thinking will become the new normal, so being able to demonstrate human intelligence will be essential when connecting with others for the greater good.

As the world faces numerous large-scale risks, possible future pandemics, climate change, and a shortage of food and resources, leaders will need to think beyond business to consider the wider implications of being human in an ever-changing world of disruption.

Leadership 5.0

Overall, leadership has been through a massive transition in the last 50 years. It has moved from industrial-style management before both World Wars, to leaders in the 60 and 70s who were selected on leadership characteristics. This has been by fuelled by the command-and-control style of leadership across organisations which we still see today. Then we had the advent of EQ in the 80s onwards which meant leaders needed to demonstrate self-awareness and emotionally connect with their people. Today, it is about value-based authentic leadership, leaders who want to make a difference, who have a sense of agency and who can demonstrate the learning agility to adapt to change.

What it means to be a leader is changing over time and leadership practice is playing catch-up with leadership theory. Leadership can be made as complex or simple as a leader wants. Understanding what good looks like and then continually practising this, is what makes the great leaders of today.

But when we look to the future with the volatility, uncertainty, change, disruption, and ambiguity that will come from the rate of technological, economic, and bio-genetic changes, along with the global challenges we will face, leadership will need to adapt quickly.

We cannot afford to continue with command-and-control styles of leadership and the younger generations coming through will not accept it. In addition, with mass automation to come, those working will want the freedom and autonomy to be leaders in their own right.

At this moment in time, we are currently still transitioning to Leadership 3.0 because of the pockets of command-and-control and transactional leadership still holding sway within organisations.

Those organisations that understand **Leadership 3.0** which is Transformational Leadership (where Leaders inspire and create followers), will be those organisations reaping the benefits from a culture and growth perspective because they will be creating higher levels of motivation and employee engagement.

Those ahead of the curve will now be moving to **Leadership 4.0.** which is Creational Leadership (where Leaders give their people the confidence and autonomy to be the leader they are).

As we move much further into the future, it will be essential to move to a much higher level of thinking about leadership, to overcome the pressures the human race will face in the future.

A move to **Leadership 5.0.**, known as Autonomous Leadership (where Leaders elevate and connect leaders who are purposeful, contextual, human-centred neuroleaders to create agile and powerful hive style leadership and make a difference in the world) will be required. As previously mentioned, leaders will also need to be creative, imaginative, intuitive, and ethical.

If we think about where we are right now with all the change resulting from the pandemic and the state of 'Future Shock' we are all starting to experience, as well as a lack of morality and ethics from global leaders and organisations across the world, then there has never been a time in need of stronger leadership based on integrity and respect. In the same way that we all go through the process of interview and deep assessment, especially for roles higher up in organisations, it is time our world leaders went through the same robust assessment to challenge their fit for the role and ensure they have the right motives and integrity to lead. The decisions that need to be made for the future are the ones we are making right now. Having a new framework and spectrum for leadership and understanding what it will take to get us there, will be a road map for success when it comes to our survival in the future.

Quick Reminder:

- An individual's psychological state due to the accelerated rate of technological, economic, and social change is leaving people 'future shocked'

- We understand that we need to be more human-centred when leading in the future, but we also need to start thinking more like AI to understand what decisions AI would make in the future.

- In the near future AI software will be able to make line management a thing of the past, with AI Management Support systems.

- Leaders in the near future will need to become change facilitators and move away from command-and-control and transactional styles of leadership, as the expectations of new generations demand greater autonomy.

- The push on leadership autonomy across the workplace will see a move away from static competency models to new models of leadership based on leadership success factors, outcomes, roles, strengths and values.

- 'Purposeful' leadership will be required in the future where leaders demonstrate how they and the business impacts the environment, society, community, customers, employees, and stakeholders.

- Leaders will need to contextualise situations in the future with critical thinking, creativity, empathy, and resilience to provide context-sensitive response to all the uncertainty and change.

- In the years to come, we are going to learn so much more about how the brain works that we will see a move to neuroleadership practice; we will see technology connect directly to the brain in the future to enhance and upgrade our capabilities.

- To ensure we are equipped and have the leaders the world now wants to see, we need to move on an advanced trajectory from Leadership 3.0 to Leadership 5.0.

- This begins with creating leaders who have a sense of morality, integrity, and respect in everything they do.

To Do:
- *Are you or your leaders or employees in a state of future shock?*

- *If line management was removed, how would you develop your leaders?*

- *Does your leadership model reflect the times we now live?*

- *Are you or your leaders purposeful in purpose and action?*

- *Do you or your leaders demonstrate contextual leadership?*

- *Are you learning about neuroscience and how the brain works to develop your leadership?*

- *You rated your leadership at the start in the first chapter - how do you move yourself, your people and organisation to the next level?*

- *How is your leadership on a trajectory to Leadership 5.0?*

The Big Idea:

The future will require new leadership - Leadership 5.0

A Leadership Lesson from the Octopus

"We split from our common ancestor with the octopus half a billion years ago. And yet, you can make friends with an octopus." – Sy Montgomery, American naturalist and author

Octopuses are molluscs, known for having eight arms and bulbous heads and live in our oceans. They have no bones and are very intelligent creatures who adapt to their surrounding and environment, especially when it comes to predators.

The octopus can change colour to camouflage itself and its texture in less than a second, blending into its surroundings with incredible accuracy. This amazing ability enables the Octopus to thrive in the deep ocean.

Biologists have found that each arm of the octopus is capable of doing different things, so the octopus is the most natural of multi-taskers on the planet. While one arm may search for food, the other is feeling and navigating the environment. It is a well-known fact that octopuses have eight arms, but did you know each arm contains its own 'mini brain'?!

In the wild, octopuses have been shown to build little dens and use stones to create a sort of shield to protect the entrance or to camouflage themselves. They are excellent problem-solvers having demonstrated a high level of intelligence and problem-solving in labs. They've also been known to escape their tanks to eat a fish in an adjacent tank and then return to their own tanks before anyone notices...

The Octopus tends to be solitary, but some have been found living together in Hives and working together. The greatest leadership lesson is that the Octopus is highly capable of adapting to its surrounding, both in the ocean and the lab, demonstrating amazing learning agility.

Habitat: Octopuses are found in every ocean of the world and along every coast of the United States. Octopuses live in coastal marine waters and spend much of their time in dens - small holes and crevices in rocks and coral.

There are around 300 species of octopus, and the numbers of octopuses in the world's seas are increasing, despite a decline in fish population.

Octopus are a lesser endangered species with only three types on the endangered list.

9
Leadership Development

Developing the Leaders of the future

The onset of virtual reality and metaverse development

> "P is positive emotion, E is engagement, R is relationships, M is meaning, and A is accomplishment. Those are the five elements of what free people chose to do. Pretty much everything else is in service of one of or more of these goals. That's the human dashboard." - Martin Seligman, American psychologist and author

Learned Helplessness in Organisations

In 1967, the concept of 'Learned Helplessness' was discovered accidentally by psychologists Martin Seligman and Steven F. Maier. Seligman initiated research on learned helplessness at the University of Pennsylvania as an extension of his interest in depression. Seligman and his colleague Maier were studying dogs who had been conditioned to expect a light electric shock if they heard a bell. They found that those dogs exposed to electric shocks in one situation where there was no escape, would not look for escape when it was possible in a different situation. The electric shock had conditioned them to give up on hope because of their past experience, where there was no escape. Normally, animals would always try to get away from negative situations or outcomes. Dogs who had not been in the negative situation of 'no escape', when placed in the new situation positively looked for a way out. The dogs already conditioned had given up hope, even in the new situation.

The experiment was replicated with human subjects which provided the same results albeit using loud noise instead of electric shocks!

This condition became known as 'learned helplessness', where both animals and humans behave in the same way once they are conditioned to expect the worse or their conditioning leaves them helpless. The impact of the negative experience on them is motivational, cognitive, and the emotional effects of uncontrollability. In his book, *Learned Helplessness* (1975), Seligman explained that due to negative experiences and conditioning, the inability to act, the lack of confidence and impact on self-esteem, along with sadness and physical illness, where all symptoms of the condition.

The theory of Learned Helplessness has been used to explain a large number of human conditions where individuals find themselves helpless, stuck, sick or addicted. As creatures of habit, we find ourselves conditioned by every experience, but in the case of learned helplessness, we can't find a way out from that conditioning. And the same sometimes can be said for organisational behaviour, when after years employees become institutionalised. This obviously is not due to electric shocks but used as a metaphor - if organisational change is deemed continually negative, then the corresponding behaviour can be one of learned helplessness. There are many people who feel stuck in their current role where they cannot advance but feel paralysed and unable to leave due to fear of the consequences.

Leadership Development

When providing leadership development, the normal question from any savvy business will be, what will be my return on investment (ROI)? With a $166 billion quoted by Forbes spent on Leadership Development in the US alone, there has to be some equitable benefit for such a large investment.

What does that $166 billion equate to?

You would agree that leadership obviously must matter, based on that investment alone. And then in turn, to the impact that leadership development would have on the bottom line of an organisation. And those focused on developing their top talent and leaders with a reasonable budget must surely be considering how they are spending their budget on leadership development. Why would that be?

• If spent well then, the return on investment will impact profitability, enhance employee engagement, and maximise results.
• If spent appropriately, it will ensure leaders can be equipped and feel empowered to deal with the 'new normal' and ensure leaders feel ready for more uncertainty and change in the future.
• It is important that a leader's mindset is developed, and a growth mindset is encouraged within the organisation.

According to research completed by Carol Dweck and Senn Delaney, organisations who develop 'learning cultures' found employees were more likely to feel a sense of ownership and commitment to the future of the company, more likely to take risks and foster innovation, and have greater trust in the company.

Especially in the times we are now living, a well-thought through leadership development strategy is essential to the success of the organisation that is responsive and aligned to business strategy. Otherwise, a reactive response to develop leaders due to external influences will mean a serious amount of time and effort wasted, where organisations quickly move to a solution and provider for little return, other than ticking the development box.

Instead, taking that step back to consider how to align clearly to the business strategy and ensuring leaders fully understand what good looks like, is the foundation for leadership development success. In effect, if you take a step back and provide the right special attention to your own strategy, there is a good possibility you will make a greater difference and move forward more quickly.

Even the more experienced organisations can be reactive to change, making quick decisions on the need to keep up with the pace of change. In an ideal world, there should always be a level of scientific data and analysis to support decisions, coupled with the intuitive understanding of moving in the right direction, rather than quickly identifying new values and leadership behaviours or what is seen as leadership gaps, without the right investigation and research.

The importance of being inclusive throughout the organisation, to include key leadership influencers and change champions or cultural architects, will help to define the development strategy and embed it within the organisation. But how many organisations get their values, behaviours and competencies mixed up, which only lead to confusion when it comes to expectations?

Whether you are an organisation who has had some success in developing leaders, or you see yourself as a well-developed organisation, it is always important to take a step back to consider if you are moving in the right direction. It is then only the sails you need to adjust, rather than the whole leadership journey and direction of the company.

"The single biggest way to impact an organisation is to focus on leadership development. There is almost no limit to the potential of an organisation that recruits good people, raises them up as leaders and continually develops them." - John Maxwell, American author and speaker

Now is the time to define leadership for your organisation, to shape your future and continue to grow during these changing and challenging times. Based on how the future will change, it is important to future-proof your leaders and ensure you have a robust and responsive leadership development strategy.

Horizontal v Vertical Leadership Development

The growth of the gig economy and pandemic is having a big impact on leaders and organisations due to short term contracts, part-time or freelance work as opposed to permanent jobs. This is driving talent acquisition to look for new types of leadership behaviours when recruiting, especially as a more human-centred approach to leadership is required. The challenge here is to bring in leaders who have the learning agility to quickly learn and make a difference.

As we progress into the future, gig leadership will become more of a norm than the anomaly so providing fast-paced development options for speed, to competency and building a cultural mindset, will be key. This is made easier when leadership development is integrated into all people-practices which means talent acquisition identifies external talent that fits the leadership mindset for the organisation.

Right people, right mindset, right time.

And identifying that talent both externally and internally is critical to an organisation's success with the complex challenges of unceasing transformation, lockdown, change, technological and digital advances, and the need to learn and adapt faster.

In his white paper for CCL, Nick Petrie explains that to develop leaders in a complex world of volatility, ambiguity and change, 'Vertical' leadership development is about transformation of the leader.

'Horizontal' development is about capability, skills, and knowledge.

'Vertical' development is about mindset, attitudes, values, and beliefs.

What is essential when recruiting and developing top talent, is ensuring a framework of 'what good looks like' for leadership is effectively in place. Bringing in leaders with a purpose-driven mindset that aligns to the organisational culture ensures ongoing transition of results and performance. Having existing leaders with the same mindset aligned to the mindset of the organisation is what will create a congruent culture and therefore support growth and profitability.

Horizontal Leadership Development	**Vertical Leadership Development**
Adding knowledge & skills	Growing abilities to think and act in complex, systematic and interdependent ways
Transmitted from experts	Earned though life experience
It's about what you think	It's about how you think
Competencies	Mindsets
Expert knowledge	Growing up, maturing
Technique	Greater perspective & transformation of consciousness

Building leadership capability is essential, but it is when the mindsets align that you will see the difference to the effectiveness and culture of your organisation.

Leadership Development Strategy

The future is changing every day and we can all make predictions as to what the future may hold. Some are more qualified than others to do so, with some having safe predictions like self-driving cars, to the more visionary such as we will all live in space and the earth will be a place we visit on holiday – this was recently stated by Amazon's Jeff Bezos to help save the planet in the future. One thing is sure, no matter where you work now or in the immediate future, organisations will continue spending millions on Leadership Development. Yes, you would think by the total money spent to date we might actually be there by now, but we know that it is an ongoing process with learning, building capability and developing potential, especially when focused on mindsets.

The current trend is that digital technology is the holy grail, employees own their own development, technology provides all the learning, so away you go and knock yourself out. Learning and Leadership Development box ticked, as we have landed the technology, it looks great, and you can't complain there is not enough stuff for you. Plus, it has AI which through machine-learning, will push out and remind you that what you said you wanted to learn can all be found through articles, video, podcasts, books and more at your own fingertips. So, we tell ourselves 'Job done' - leadership development and learning truly boxed off for the future generations to come…now let's get back to the real business stuff we should be focused on. And we have the awards to prove we are a learning organisation; what more could our employees or leaders ask for?

But we all know there is so much more to developing leaders and our employees.

The essence of having a growth mindset is about continual learning and that is what the new AI machine-learning powered technology is helping to support and provide some amazing platforms that help leaders grow. One of the challenges in the future will be to know which is the best platform to use, as they are now popping up more and more with providers now looking to capitalise on the market.

The 2018 State of Leadership Development Report from Harvard Business Publishing, it found that millennials are more critical of L&D programmes citing that they lack innovation, are not relevant and should be using well-sourced content to address the strategic needs of the business. They are looking for a more responsive, innovative, and credible development approach compared to a one size fits all. And that was before the pandemic! Additionally, they will also now want flexibility in how they learn so more typically, virtually and from home.

Let's explore different types of Leadership Development and you can assess where your organisation currently resides based on the descriptions below…

The Reactive LD Strategy
This type of organisation has developed leaders historically by building what the business wants. There is no set LD strategy; as HR has supported the business, LD has grown reactively but because it has been over some time, it is viewed more organically. The business requests a meeting and drives the agenda, HR goes away with a 'to do' list and looks to provide solutions in house firstly, or then looks for the best external provider to plug the skill gap. Occasionally there will be a flagship leadership programme driven out by one of the Executive team based on an event or speaker they have seen, but delivered then by the Learning or LD team within HR. There will be pocket industries found across the company doing different things, so it can get frustrating that what is being provided is not always connected to the bigger picture and is for short term results.

The Static LD Strategy

This type of organisation has taken the time to build a leadership framework or model. There will be clear competencies or leadership behaviours. There will be various ways to learn as a leader and it will be linked back to the leadership model. Through your performance conversations based on how you rated, you will have development actions or a plan of competencies you will need to develop. Therefore, based on your performance conversation, you can now easily help yourself by going through the LMS or Intranet to be able to self-serve and attend the development options the company provides. The options are blended, and the company provides a wide range of learning opportunities. This is the static model of leadership development; once in place there may be Executive or Senior Leader development, but everyone else self-serves and owns their own development.

The Digital LD Strategy

This type of organisation has run to digital or is already a digital organisation. The belief here is that technology can provide all learning and leadership needs for individuals, no matter their learning preference. Digital is the future, and it is all encompassing plus it will measure and track your learning. This organisation provides digital self-service solutions but little else in the form of meaningful development, unless there is an urgent need that the digital solutions are unable to provide but they will still be directed to some self-directed learning as part of process. The 'Netflix' approach to leadership development is seen as the way forwards.

The Responsive LD Strategy

This type of organisation will ensure that they have aligned their business strategy and desired culture to their leadership development. They will have considered what good looks like for leadership and defined it for their leaders, ensuring all leaders understand the organisation's leadership success factors. There will be a clear leadership development strategy-built year on year, that is responsive

> to the needs of leaders to build capability based on these leadership success factors. There will be a blended range of solutions, with self-directed digital solutions being only one option provided to leaders. What is provided is collaborative and in time develops throughout the year through communication, events providing external thinking, internal social media content and experiential learning. The responsive approach ensures leadership development is a vehicle to embed the desired culture and to future-proof leaders.

When you look at your organisation, which of these LD Strategies do you recognise, and which do you need to move towards?

Organisations need to move to a form of responsive leadership development instead of static offerings. This will ensure leaders get 'in the moment' development with what is topical or what the business is focused on at the time through the business strategy. Responsive employees and experiential leaders are more likely to engage and therefore learn to develop behaviours which in turn impacts your ROI.

Creating a Responsive LD Strategy

When it comes to having a responsive leadership development strategy, there are a number of factors to take into consideration:

Guiding Principles

Firstly, you need your LD Strategy to be aligned to the business strategy through a set of guiding principles. These may be as simple as principles such as being aligned to the business strategy and values, based around leadership model behaviours, innovative in approach, providing choice to leaders instead of being mandated, future focused and creating strategic thinkers.

These principles are important because they act as the philosophy for the strategy.

As part of those guiding principles, it is good to also create PERMA – this is what Martin Seligman calls the five elements of what free people choose to do.

1. P is positive emotion - ensure your strategy will create positive emotion for leaders through your leadership interventions and objectives.

2. E is engagement - how you communicate and engage through a clear comms plan, but also to think through the narrative you will tell.

3. R is relationships - how you provide the opportunity to collaborate and network as part of your strategy.

4. M is meaning - as part of the narrative you create, think about what sense of meaning and purpose will leaders have as part of your LD Strategy and interventions.

5. And finally, A is accomplishment - what sense of achievement will your leaders experience from putting ideas into practice, to making a difference, to becoming qualified or recognised for their efforts.

This is what Martin Seligman calls his "Human Dashboard", which are five brilliant guidelines for helping to create your strategy. The whole essence of these guiding principles is then embedded, from CEO and Execs, throughout the design and execution of your strategy, as well as giving a deeper understanding for what it is based on to the project team who deliver the strategy. This will then echo and become embedded through each intervention and ensure it drives towards the desired culture, optimising results and building your leadership capability.

Competencies, Mindsets & Success Factors

Another important factor will be to design your strategy, programmes, and interventions around your leadership model. There are lots of different ways to design your model dependent upon the culture and outcomes you want. Whatever version you decide upon, it is super important because it describes what good looks like for leaders. The best way to embed that model and driven real understanding is to get leaders to assess themselves against the model's competencies, mindsets, or success factors, to identify strengths and development areas. Then ensure your LD Strategy provides leaders with a choice of blended, innovative, experiential, and responsive solutions they can choose from based on the Success Factors. This is key to developing your leadership DNA and future-proofing your leadership capability.

Experiential and Immersive Development

To develop leaders and drive real behavioural change, it is essential to provide real time immersive and experiential leadership development opportunities. Bringing leaders from across the business together in groups to work on leadership challenges, use of mentoring, learning sets and team building all provide experiential opportunities. When you bring people together, the level of creativity, teamwork and commitment from groups looking to overcome challenges drives behavioural change. It is experienced and felt in the moment. These experiences are what really drive behavioural change, along with helping leaders to think differently. As already stated, if you want to change behaviour you have to change the thinking behind that behaviour. Experiential and immersive leadership development is one of the ways along with providing in-time responsive content to shape thinking.

Social Media - Collaborative – Social Learning

Using a social media platform to support your offering helps to embed responsive and collaborative thinking by tapping into diversity of thought. Whatever the programme, intervention, or event, you can provide inspirational and thought- provoking content to support it. When you use your CEO or Executives as sponsors and content providers, not only does it raise the visibility and credibility, but it also connects the organisation from top down and bottom up. You can also use your Leadership Influencers and Cultural Architects to post great content and support others' content with encouraging comments. Bringing in speakers and asking them to post or do a Q&A results in increased uptake, exposure and sharing of external content to drive a different level of thinking. If you don't have a social media platform or strategy, then you need to understand you are missing a big stepping stone to the future of metaverse leadership development.

Psychometric & 360 – Developing Self Awareness

It goes without saying that if you want to have leaders equipped and enabled for the future, then it is essential to develop their self-awareness. The best way of doing this to provide insight and development based on objective data using psychometrics or 360 tools. To maximise the use of these tools, work with your external partner to adapt them around your leadership model behaviours to connect the thinking, so leaders can understand how the psychometric or 360 relates to leadership and your organisation. Consider then how you keep the psychology, types and traits alive across the organisation, to make it a common language based on shared data and understanding. When you work in an organisation who has completely embedded the tool, it becomes like a second language.

The greatest successes come when previous difficult relationships have been worked through because of an appreciation of combined strengths and differences.

Self Service – Instant Learning

As already mentioned above, this should be a massive part of your LD Strategy to provide 'in the moment' learning for your leaders and employees. In developing your leadership once again, map solutions such as books, articles, videos and Ted talks to the behaviours of your leadership model. Where I have seen this work best is when you have solutions mapped to the leadership model for basic, intermediate, and advanced levels, ensuring that leaders look to stretch strengths and develop weaker or development areas. Platforms now provide the kind of AI that recognises your needs and pushes key learning content to you. In many successful organisations this is provided to support career development and literally has solutions mapped to all possible career pathways.

There are many other ways to develop leaders from Learning Sets that provide on- the-job learning and feedback mechanisms, assessment of top talent, talent development, business schools, qualifications, leadership programmes and events or speakers to provide external thinking.

Leadership development should not be restricted to those who are C-suite or one or two levels down. Everyone within the organisation is a leader, so you need to ensure that you provide the right leadership model that factors in all levels and then provides the best options for development. Yes, a much greater percentage of the budget will be spent at C-suite and for senior leaders, but it about ensuring that everyone has the option to develop as a leader. If you are building your LD Strategy, be sure to focus on a responsive and immersive strategy in readiness for the future.

Leadership Development of the Future

When we think about the future, we need to understand what the top skills will be that we will need to develop. Based on the World Economic Forum findings, the top ten skills of 2025 will be:

- Analytical thinking & innovation
- Active learning and learning strategies
- Complex problem-solving
- Critical thinking and analysis
- Creativity, originality, and initiative
- Leadership and social influence
- Technology use, monitoring and control
- Technology design and programming
- Resilience, stress tolerance and flexibility
- Reasoning, problem-solving and ideation

As we mentioned earlier, as work becomes more automated what will set us apart will be human creativity, critical thinking, and our imagination. The onset of more advanced technology will see ways to develop leaders through immersive virtual reality, advanced AI, the organisation's own version of metaverse and augmentation.

Imagine recruiting new leaders and being able to give them the full experience of leading a team through virtual reality, and the coaching assistant to be able stop, start and continue at key moments in their immersive experience. Or the new Executive who can practice presentations with questions from the board in a fully immersive board experience virtual reality set. Or being on a leadership course with avatars of the greatest leaders in our time so attending an out of bounds teamworking course in the internal metaverse with Alexander the Great, Batman, Carl Jung and Abraham Maslow providing the in-time lessons as you work through the tasks with them! When you do go into the office and walk down the corridor, the leadership hologram that greets you and can pick up on all your vital signs, will calmly provide advice for you on your journey to your next meeting. When working from home, being sat round a table with the augmented holograms of your team in the internal metaverse. The possibilities are endless…

There is so much to come with technology that will transcend the boundaries of what we would now class as the new normal. We are only just touching the surface with hybrid and smart working, with so much more to come in the near future.

The limitless possibilities will need to be designed so the development experience and then resulting transfer in behavioural change come first, with the technology to support it, rather than the other way round. When we think of all of the possibilities for new types of development, it will still be important to have a leadership model framework and a clear move towards Leadership 5.0 as critical foundations for developing the leaders of the future.

Organisational Conditioning

So, we return back to Martin Seligman's theory of Learned Helplessness because it is so easy for leaders to become a victim of organisational conditioning. For all the fancy development to come, if we don't recognise that leaders and employees can become stuck due to the organisation's default settings, then development with bells and whistles doesn't really matter. By actually thinking about what it means to be human, organisations will start to be able to understand how previously they may have created an unsavoury environment or a place that people feel/felt trapped in. The opportunity to learn from those organisations that have a growth mindset and an environment where people are treated like adults rather than children will need to be grasped and the consideration of what type of human being you really want your organisations to be.

When we look back to hunter-gatherer times and the practice of 'Hive' leadership, have we actually just missed the point all these years, as we now transcend into a future that recognises that this may be the way forward, as leadership transforms?

Quick Reminder:
- 'Learned Helplessness' is where humans or animals behave the same way once they are conditioned to expect the worse, or their conditioning leaves them helpless.

- With $166 billion quoted by Forbes spent on Leadership Development in the US alone, it not only points to the importance of leaders but also the question around return on investment.

- Organisations who develop 'learning cultures' according to research, found employees are more likely to feel a sense of ownership and commitment to the future of the company, more likely to take risks and foster innovation, and have greater trust in the company.

- 'Horizontal' leadership development is about capability, skills, and knowledge.

- 'Vertical' leadership development is about mindset, attitudes, values, and beliefs.

- Building leadership capability is essential but it is when the mindsets align that you will see the difference to the effectiveness and culture of your organisation.

- There are four different examples of types of Leadership Development Strategy: 1. Reactive, 2. Static 3. Digital 4. Responsive.

- Responsive LD Strategy is the recommended approach as the model for leadership development strategy.

- As we move into the future, we will need to identify the critical skills that need developing and ensure that development interventions are designed content-led first instead of technology-led.

- There will be an array of different technological development solutions which will stretch the boundaries of our imagination and provide new ways of learning for leaders.

- Organisations need to face down on their organisational conditioning, and it is another reason to focus on the mindset of an organisation.

To Do:
- *Are you or your leaders in a place of learned helplessness?*
- *Do you get a return on investment (ROI) from your leadership development?*
- *Do you have a learning culture?*
- *Do you ensure your leaders receive both horizontal and vertical leadership development?*
- *What type of LD strategy do you have, if any… Reactive, Static, Digital, or Responsive?*
- *How can you develop your LD Strategy and make it responsive?*
- *How can you create guiding principles and use PERMA?*
- *How are you incorporating new technologies into your leadership development?*
- *What is your organisational conditioning and how can defining the mindset of your organisation help you to move away from negative conditioning for your people?*

The Big Idea:

As we move into the future, we will need to develop the leadership skills that set us apart from AI, robotics, and automation through 'Responsive' Leadership Development.

The Leadership Lesson from Humans

"Before you call yourself a Christian, Buddhist, Muslim, Hindu or any other theology, learn to be human first." — Shannon L. Alder, American therapist and author

Human being, a culture-bearing primate classified in the genus Homo, especially the species Homo Sapiens. Human beings are related to great apes but have a far more advanced brain, with a higher level of reasoning and speech.

Humans are the most widespread and have the greatest numbers of species of primate but differ due to their bipedalism and intelligence. Because of this, Human beings have designed and developed advanced tools, language, society and culture.

What really separates them from other animal species is their ability for complex reasoning and communication, along with their ability to solve difficult problems and have deep introspection about life.

Human beings have an innate ability to be able to work together on groups, teams and across societies. They are able to inspire, motivate and empower others to achieve tasks but on the flip side, can cause arguments with deeply held beliefs causing differentiation, conflict and at times war.

Although Human beings could be viewed as superior to animals and although blessed with large amounts of empathy and reasoning, they are more likely to be self-destructive towards their own species.

Habitat: Found in cities, farmlands, savannahs, and most locations across the globe and also through their ingenuity in space.

7.9 billion Human beings (and counting!) can be found on Earth.

Nearly a quarter of all deaths worldwide are linked to environmental issues. That's 12.6 million deaths every year, according to the World Health Organisation (WHO). "Human beings really are the most important endangered species," said Margaret Chan, previous Director General of the WHO.

The Four Riders of the Apocalypse are known to be a direct cause of Human beings' activity in the world.

10
Beyond Leadership

Leadership

The leaders the world now needs to see

"The fact remains that man has unprecedented control over the world and everything in it. And so, whether he likes it or not, what happens next is very largely up to him." – Sir David Attenborough, broadcaster and naturalist.

Dysfunctional Leadership

At the end of the 2021 Formula One Grand Prix season, both Lewis Hamilton and Max Verstappen where vying for the position of World Champion. The final race, the Abu Dhabi Grand Prix, ended in controversy as Lewis Hamilton, with six laps to go, was close to 12 seconds ahead of Max and with all things being normal, was to be crowned World Champion for a record 8th time. However, what we witnessed watching the race was Lewis Hamilton being completely robbed of his 8th World Title. How was he robbed? By the dysfunctional leadership of Race Director and key decision-maker Michael Masi making several major errors of judgement, as the FIA has now officially reported.

With six laps to go, one of the drivers, Nicholas Latifi, crashed and the safety car was sent out on the track. Red Bull brought Verstappen in for a third time to go to the softs, with Mercedes unable to bring Hamilton in as it would have meant sacrificing the lead.

Based on the rules of Formula One, all of the cars, including the five Lewis had to pass to be so far ahead of Max, should have passed the safety car before the race proceeded. Instead, Masi decided, for reasons known only to himself, to 're-interpret' the rules and only remove the 5 lapped cars between Lewis and Max. This meant that Max was able to restart next to Lewis Hamilton, wiping out Lewis' 12-second lead, and on faster tyres guaranteeing Max the World Title. Lewis had the same tyres but Max had a certain winning advantage because he had been able to pit to faster 'soft' tyres.

If Michael Masi had followed the rules, it would have taken the remaining laps for all the cars to pass the safety car, meaning Lewis would and should have been World Champion. Of course, that would not have been the greatest of ends to the race or world title, but Lewis would have won anyway if the race had continued as normal had there been no crash. Michael Masi broke the rules and demonstrated extremely poor leadership supposedly for the 'good of racing' by also changing his mind just before the final lap final lap after what looked like a conversation with certain 'interested' parties.

Now, I'm all for breaking the rules to think differently, to create new ways of thinking or doing new things, but in this case, Michael displayed dysfunctional leadership. And how the lap was not disqualified after the race also smacks of a dysfunctional organisation in the FIA itself. In my view, this was daylight robbery of Lewis Hamilton's 8th World Title and placed the FIA in a very compromising position in front of millions watching around the world.

Imagine it is the football World Cup Final and the two teams draw, and it goes to extra time and the ref decides that one team can only have 5 players while the other can keep their 11 on the pitch.

I hear you saying, 'That is absolutely ridiculous!' and yes, it is, but that is the equivalent of what happened to Lewis Hamilton. Max Verstappen recently said of himself with ongoing complete lack of self-awareness, 'I deserved to be world champion'. Yes Max, you raced superbly all season but actually you deserved to finish Runner-up, because you got the equivalent of 11 men on the last lap to Lewis's 5, which should never have been allowed.

The amount of bias towards Max on social media meant that for some reason there were two views to the situation. Actually, there were not two views if you examine this objectively and never should have been. Unfortunately, it has become acceptable in society to be morally hijacked by events, political parties, and leaders. Michael Masi was later sacked as Race Director but not after ensuring one of the most controversial endings to a sporting event in the history of sport.

Now of course, this example is nothing compared to the dysfunctional leadership of Vladimir Putin's war crimes currently happening in Ukraine, but I wanted to use the above as a clear example of dysfunctional leadership.

Masi's decision should have been corrected, Hamilton given his 8th World title and Masi should have been sacked or disciplined at the time rather than 3 months later. If you or I got it so wrong working for an organisation, what do you think would have happened? Sorry Max Verstappen fans, it is nothing personal! He is a great driver, but he should not be world champion. I understand all about who has the fastest car and other decisions through the season and so on but I'm purely talking in this instance of Masi's very poor and ridiculous decision in the moment.

What is really unfortunate is that in the moment, Michael didn't think about what was the right thing to do. This is why it is so important in life that as leaders we are always taking decisions based on our values and what is right.

A Moral Compass

A leader needs an internal moral compass that guides them in their moments of pressure and challenge. This compass is based on your values, principles, and sense of morality. Part of the compass and within your values is a human focus on compassion, empathy, kindness and understanding. It allows you as a leader to be your very best. Floyd Woodrow, formerly of the SAS and now a business leader explains in his book, *The Strategist, The Warrior and You* that to be a great leader, you need a compass that firstly has a North Star. Your North Star is your ultimate goal and the difference you are going to make in the world. Then to the east are your values and who you really are, so the leader you want to be. South is your strategy for getting to your North Star. It is in effect your plan and map with all the steps on the way to achieving your ultimate goal. And west is your Warrior, which really stands for your inner mental and physical resilience. Floyd talks about the importance of each of these cardinal points with organisations, business leaders and in schools.

Having this guiding moral compass provides a foundation for being a great leader. In both Michael Masi's and Vladimir Putin's case, unfortunately their moral compass as leaders is truly broken. The thing about being a good or great leader is that you are there to help and serve others, rather than your own corrupt agenda.

So, the advice here is to work out firstly what your North Star is and define it clearly. Next, create a plan or map of how you are going to get there. Then ensure you are both mentally and physically in the best shape you can be and finally, be true to your values and principles in being the best leader you can be. This may take a little bit of creative thinking so think big! Draw your North Star, and create your map, make it physical and bright so you have something to use for visualisation and to continually refer to. Now, talking about creativity and North Stars...

Leaders and Organisations that make a Difference

In 1968, NASA commissioned Dr. George Land, Professor of the University of Minnesota, to design a highly specialised "divergent thinking" creativity test. They wanted to explore and try to better understand the true source of creativity. He went on to test 1,600 five-year-olds and 98% of the children scored at the "creative genius" level! He then went on to do a longitudinal study, testing the same group of kids 5 and 10 years later. What did he find out?

At the age of 10, only 30% of the children scored at the same level and at 15, it was only 12%. So from the age of 5 to the age of 15, children scored 86% worse in creativity. He then went to test Adults and find out if it reduced further, so they administered the same test to 280,000 adults (25+ years old) and only 2% scored at Genius Level, a massive drop! So in 96% of adults who may have scored at Genius Level at the age of 5, creativity levels had incredibly dropped. This does not mean that those adults were not creative at all, but their capability had diminished.

Why is that?

And the reason is because as we grow into adulthood we are conditioned and conform to look for the right answer to any problem or question. This means we have lost our ability to think laterally to problems because we have been trained by our life experience to think logically and rationally. This helps us to survive in the world, which is essential to our survival, however it does mean our capacity for creativity diminishes over the years, to the point that many people will actually say they are not creative which is really a lack of self-awareness. There are lots of different ways to be creative, we are creative as Human Beings.

As we already know from earlier, creativity will be critical to our future and our ability to think differently about the world's problems. When we now think about those problems such as the pandemic, climate change, automation, war, terrorism, scarcity of resources, rapid urbanisation, and the increasing and aging population, there has never been a more important time to use our creative problem-solving skills and collaboration as a species if we want to survive in the future. There is now an opportunity for leadership to go beyond what we would call the line of duty, to really consider how leaders and leadership adds value to the bigger picture to make a difference in the world.

When we look at the largest leadership consultancies around the world, we find that sustainability is at the core of what they now do, what they have proven to add value to their business and how they now advise clients.

As Deloitte states in their whitepaper, *2030 Purpose: Good business and a better future*, "Businesses can make a huge impact towards the achievement of the UN Sustainable Development Goals and the good news is that this isn't just good for humanity, it's good for business... Based on their research, it's not just compatible, it's inter-dependent: a commitment to sustainable development positively impacts all stakeholder perspectives.

This inter-dependency cannot be incidental, it needs to place at the heart of the business, enshrined in the purpose of the organisation."

And at the heart of those businesses need to be leaders who role model, live the values and pave the way for a more sustainable future.

As large successful leadership and outplacement consultancy in the UK 10Eighty state in their whitepaper, *The Rise of the Human-Focused Leader*, "'And Beyond' Leadership – going beyond the immediate; broadening and reaching out to those outside the inner circle and the function; being inclusive, either in new ways of thinking, collaborating with competitors or in dealing with employees; taking a collective leadership approach." Based on their research, expectations of leaders are to now think beyond the work environment to, "All leaders now have to demonstrate a view on Environmental, Social and Governance issues as well as the actions they are taking. Areas included diversity and inclusion, pollution, climate change, generational differences and adapting to ever-changing workforce dynamics."

This has led many organisations and businesses to have clear sustainable objectives and strategic goals in place to demonstrate how they are helping make the world a better place. This has been found to benefit organisations i.e., if a cup of coffee was the same blend and price in two coffee shops, people are more likely to shop in the coffee shop that supports good causes such as the UN Global Goals than the coffee shop that doesn't, even if it was slightly more expensive.

And organisations can now use technology platforms such as the B1G1 platform for good causes which in itself is like the 'Amazon for Kindness'. You pay a monthly membership and then any money that is given towards good causes goes straight to them. As we know with many charities this is not the case, and out of every pound given it is pennies that eventually find their way to the cause.

Korn Ferry have recently stated that the role and purpose of business in society is evolving. Customers, investors, and employees are demanding that companies play a more active role in social change and that the role of the Chief Sustainability Officer has never been more important and essential for organisations of today. Korn Ferry interviewed more than 50 CEOs and CSOs in organisations around the world, to understand the role sustainability now plays in their operations, strategy, culture, and leadership. Their findings show that we now live at a time which is the tipping point for sustainability as a business imperative. To build future resilience, organisations need a CSO to drive strategy and change, along with it being an imperative way of doing business in the future.

McKinsey & Co aspire to be an impact partner and advisor on sustainability, climate, energy transition, and environmental, social, and governance (ESG) from the board room to the engine room, working with clients to lead a wave of innovation and economic growth that safeguards our planet and advances sustainability.

As we face off into the future, it is not only human existence but all living beings on the planet whose lives are at stake. As Sir David Attenborough has said, *"It's surely our responsibility to do everything within our power to create a planet that provides a home not just for us, but for all life on Earth."*

Hence why this book is threaded throughout with leadership lessons from some of the greatest land and seas creatures of the Earth, as it is our responsibility to do everything in our power to ensure their safety. It is important that we do not lose touch with the rest of the animal kingdom. Just like our past history, these animals can teach us so much about being a leader and what leadership means, along with the importance of also thinking Beyond Leadership.

We now need the leaders of tomorrow today, we need leaders who not only empower people but create leaders, and as a species we need to swiftly move along the leadership spectrum to Leadership 5.0, along with organisations and leaders who think beyond leadership. A key critical behaviour that leaders will need is the accountability to always look at themselves first before they look at others. If there is a failure by individuals, the department, or organisation, then what could they have done differently to ensure a better outcome? If the world has problems which we have explored what can leaders do to really make a difference?

In the future we will also need to be more human than the AI and robots that will simulate what it is like to be human. This deeper understanding of what it means to be a human being and to have a deeper level of kindness, humility and empathy will be critical as well as taking responsibility for our world and all life within our world. And the importance of collaboration and the reinvention of hive style leadership and leaders who are egoless but able to adapt to the cause as required. Let's face it, in the future there may not be the need for leadership because the way we interface into the world may look completely different. But until we get there, and the paradigm of leadership is redundant, then it is essential we continue in the most humane way possible if we are to survive.

The world is changing every day and it is up to us and the leaders of this world to ensure it is a much better place. That we break with our past conditioning to move past command-and-control, war mongering, coercive and dog-like behaviour to finally realise our full potential. It is a time for the spirit of creativity, innovation, and the re-invention of humankind - perhaps through renewed focus on leadership, we can survive and thrive in the future. Our ultimate North Star.

> "Savour your existence. Live every moment. Do not waste a breath."

– Nando Parrado, leader of the famous plane crash survival in the Andes in 1972.

Quick Reminder

- There is no room for dysfunctional leadership in the future if we are to transcend the times we now live and keep a pace with the rate of change.

- To be a great leader it is essential to have a moral compass which in Floyd Woodrow's case has a North Star, who you are, a Strategy and Warrior focus on your resilience.

- It is essential that organisations, businesses, and leaders identify their own North Star that relates to making a difference in the world.

- Organisations are now focused on sustainable goals because it not only makes a difference in the world, but it also makes a positive difference to business outcomes and profitability.

- Beyond Leadership is our ability as leaders to think beyond ourselves for the greater good of humankind.

- We need to move to Leadership 5.0 as quickly as we can if we are to survive in the future.

To Do:

- *Identify your own, your business', and your organisation's North Star.*
- *Consider what it means to be a 'Beyond' Leadership leader.*
- *Make a difference in the world.*

The Big Idea:

Beyond Leadership - where we see the leaders the world now needs to see making a difference in the world.

References and Further Reading

Books and Journals:

Adair, John, *How to Grow Leaders: – the seven principles of effective leadership development,* Kogan Page, (2005)

Adair, John, *Great Leaders: Inspirational Lessons in Leadership,* Thorogood Publishing, (2020)

Bass, Bernard M., *Leadership and Performance Beyond Expectations*, The Free Press, (1985)

Burns, James MacGregor, *Leadership*, Harper Collins, (1978)

Covey Stephen, *Seven Habits of Highly Effective People*, The Free Press, (1989)

Drucker, Peter, *On the Profession of Management,* Harvard Business Review Press, (1998)

Fiedler, Fred, *A Theory of Leadership Effectiveness,* New York: McGraw-Hill, (1967)

Freedman Jonathan and Sears, David, *Social Psychology*, Prentice Hall, (1981)

Garcia, Hector and Miralles, Francesc, *Ikigai: The Japanese Secret to a Long and Happy Life,* Hutchinson, *(2017)*

George, Bill, *Authentic Leadership: Rediscovering the Secrets to Creating Lasting Value,* Jossey Bass, (2003)

Goldsmith, Marshall, Lyons, Laurence, and Freas, Alyssa, *Coaching for Leadership: How the World's Greatest Coaches Help Leaders Learn,* Jossey Bass, (2020)

Goleman, Daniel, McKee, Annie and Boyatzis, Richard, *Realizing the Power of Emotional Intelligence*, Harvard Business Review Press, (2002)

Harari, Yuval Noah, *Homo Deus – a Brief History of Tomorrow*, Vintage, (2017)

Hernez-Broome, Gina and Hughes, Richard, *Leadership Development: Past, Present and Future*, Human Resource Planning Journal, (2012)

Hunt-Davis, Ben, and Beveridge, Harriet, *Will It Make the Boat Go Faster?*, Matador, (2020)

Kotter, John P, *On What Leaders Really Do*, Harvard Business Review Press, (1999)

Kouzes, James M & Posner, Barry Z, *The Leadership Challenge: How to Make Extraordinary Things Happen in Organizations*, Jossey Bass, (1995)

Landsberger Henry, *Hawthorne Revisited*, Cornell University, (1958)

McGregor, Douglas, *The Human Side of Enterprise*, McGraw Hill Higher Education, (1960)

Manville, Brook & Ober, Josiah, *A Company of Citizens: What the World's First Democracy Teaches Leaders About Creating Great Organizations*, Harvard Business Review Press, (2003)

Peltier, Bruce, *The Psychology of Executive Coaching*, Routledge, (2010)

Peters, Tom and Waterman Jr, Robert H, *In Search of Excellence: Lessons From America's Best-Run Companies*, Profile Books, (2004)

Michael E Porter, *Competitive Advantage*, Free Press, (1985)

Rosenthal, Robert and Jacobson, Lenore, *Pygmalion in the Classroom: teacher expectation and pupils' intellectual development* Holt, Rinehart and Winston, (1968)

Rosenthal, Robert & Babad, Elisha. Y. *Pygmalion in the Gymnasium.* Journal of Cases in Educational Leadership, Volume 43, (1985)

Schein, Edgar, *Organizational Culture and Leadership*, Jossey Bass, (1995)

Seligman, Martin, *Learned Helplessness*, Annual Review of Medicine, Volume 23, (1972)

Spencer, Herbert, *The Study of Sociology*, Henry S. King and Co, (1873)

Greta Thunberg, *No One Is Too Small to Make a Difference*, Penguin, (2019)

Toffler Alvin, *Future Shock*, Bodley Head, (1970)

Woodrow, Floyd *The Strategist, The Warrior and You,* Elliott and Thompson, (2016)

Websites:

10Eighty **www.10eighty.co.uk**

Korn Ferry - https://www.kornferry.com/insights/briefings-magazine/issue-25/where-well-work

World Economic Forum **www.weforum.org** Future of Job Reports 2020, World Economic Forum

TED Talks:

Eddie Obeng Talk: "World After Midnight"

Dr. Fred Johnson: "I am Enough"

Studies:

ADP study, 2019
https://uk.adp.com/resources/adp-articles-and-insights/articles/w/workforce-view-2019.aspx

CCL (Centre for Creative Leadership), white paper *Beyond Doing Good*, 2022

DDI Global Leadership Forecast, 2021

Deloitte white paper, *2030 Purpose: Good business and a better future*

Gartner, *The War for Talent*, 2020

McKinsey & Co, *War for Talent* Global survey, 2012

NeuroLeadership Institute (NLI) interviews, March 2020

Pivot Leadership (Korn Ferry), *The Third Wave*, 2019

Printed in Poland
by Amazon Fulfillment
Poland Sp. z o.o., Wrocław
04 November 2022

0d40d193-6ab4-4a98-bba0-b61dc928dacfR01